The
Complete Book of Offensive
Basketball Drills

GAME-CHANGING
DRILLS FROM AROUND
THE WORLD

GIORGIO GANDOLFI

New York Chicago San Francisco Lisbon London Madrid Mexico City
Milan New Delhi San Juan Seoul Singapore Sydney Toronto

The *McGraw·Hill* Companies

Dedicated to my late parents,
Tina and Antonio Gandolfi

1 2 3 4 5 6 7 8 9 10 11 12 13 14 15 16 17 18 19 20 21 22 23 24 25   DOC/DOC   0 9

ISBN   978-0-07-163586-8
MHID   0-07-163586-6

Art Manager: Lisa Cavallini
Illustrator: Raffaele Imbrogno

McGraw-Hill books are available at special quantity discounts to use as premiums and sales promotions or for use in corporate training programs. To contact a representative, please e-mail us at bulksales@mcgraw-hill.com.

Contents

FOREWORD

Long before basketball went worldwide and names like Dirk, Yao, Nash, and Manu became commonplace, Giorgio Gandolfi was building bridges between hoops-loving people on different continents. This rich treasury of offensive basketball wisdom is essential for the library of all coaches and players who want to maximize their understanding of this beguiling game.

No part of the globe has a corner on sound, savvy basketball knowledge, and Gandolfi offers a truly global sampling of the finest thinking on how to attack the basket or get a shot off against a tough defender. Whether it's the half-court rigor of the American college or high school coach in teaching how to get free for a shot, or the NBA mentor's knack for finding mismatches and exploiting isolations with pinpoint passing, or the fast break and dribbling drills of the Yugoslavs and Argentines, or the perimeter and inside player development secrets of the Spanish, you'll find examples here.

As he assembled this collection over decades of visiting coaches, camps, clinics, and practice sessions around the world, and breaking down videos and DVDs, Gandolfi ultimately didn't care whether the offensive drill originated with a big international name or a small club coach, or someone in between.

If it's effective in helping a coach to improve his players' pull-up jump shot or make a power move to the basket, it's here. Gandolfi has done the game a huge service—and made Planet Basketball a more intimate place—with this timely and invaluable book.

Alexander Wolff, *Sports Illustrated* senior writer and author
of *Big Game, Small World: A Basketball Adventure*

KEY TO DIAGRAMS

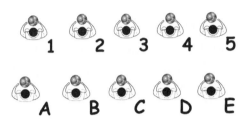

1 2 3 4 5

A B C D E

Offensive players

Defensive players

P

Passer

R

Rebounder

- - - - →

Pass

=

Hand-off pass

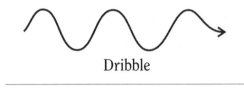

Dribble

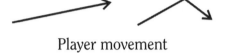

Player movement

Shot

Screen or pick

Chair

Cone

1 2 3 4 5

Court spots

1
Premises
and Suggestions

T
he Complete Book of Offensive Basketball Drills: Game-Changing Drills from around

the World is totally devoted to offensive drills. A generally held opinion is that defense

is more important than offense. "Defense wins the games and the championships."
This opinion seems to be true at all levels, from high school to the NBA to the Euroleague, the
European championship for clubs. However, in this book, we would like to give you an array of
offensive drills, which we consider to be of equal importance in winning games and championships. In this chapter, we will evaluate different aspects of drills and give some simple suggestions for choosing the drills that can help your players and, consequently, your team, to improve. If you think it's simple to choose a drill for a certain practice or to improve your players'
skill, read the following before you decide.

Why Do You Choose a Drill?

- Is it only to impress your players with your knowledge?

  *Wrong: They need drills that suit their skills, ones that will be effective in helping them
  improve individually and as a team.*

- Is it because a drill was used by a famous and winning coach?

  Fine: But are you sure that the level of the competition, as well as the size, the physical condition, the skills of your players, and your philosophy on offense, are suitable for that drill?

- Do you choose a certain drill just to break the boredom of a practice?

  Fine: But, more important, the drill must be useful and have a specific purpose or purposes.

The Art of Choosing Drills

You are starting to plan your practice. You decide to run drills that cover certain fundamentals and some game situations. That's great. But are you sure that you have evaluated the many different technical aspects tied to a drill? Choosing drills for a practice is not a simple task. On the contrary, we will show you that there is more than one detail to consider when you decide to adopt a certain drill. Consider the following:

Plan a Drill

Do not run a drill if you do not have time to evaluate it. Instead, consider exactly why, when, and how you want to run a certain drill and how it fits your daily, weekly, and monthly schedule.

Mix Fundamentals and Conditioning

Basketball is a demanding sport. Try to create a drill with the proper mix of fundamentals and conditioning. This allows the players to execute the fundamentals as well at the end of the game as they do early on.

Remember, a well-conditioned team can beat a more skilled but less-conditioned opponent.

Incorporate Competition

Competition is the heart of basketball. Try to incorporate competition in a drill whenever possible. In a drill the player can compete:

- Against the clock, when the coach must check how many shots or repetitions of a movement a player makes for a determined period of time.
- Against a teammate, both in a game-situation drill, or in a contest between two players or one team against another.

Run Drills at Game Speed

First of all, a player must master the movement—either a pass, a dribble, a shot, or other individual or collective fundamental. Then, after he is comfortable with that fundamental, he must run that drill at game speed and under game conditions, such as with a defender or in a clock situation.

Avoid Drills with Few Repetitions

Do not adopt a drill when too many players must stand and wait to make repetitions. If this happens, they will make fewer repetitions, which is detrimental to their improvement and generates a lack of intensity.

Increase Grade of Difficulty

Do not immediately run a drill with a high grade of difficulty, but instead start gradually. Then, when the players have mastered the proper routine and technique, run drills tougher than game situations, without forgetting the level of your competition, as well as the skills of your players.

Avoid Back-to-Back Demanding Drills

Do not run demanding drills one after the other. This may be effective when the players are at the peak of their physical condition, but, normally, after a very demanding and vigorous drill, it's better to run a less-strenuous one.

5

Monitor Time

Each drill must be efficient, and that efficiency is also determined by the length of the drill. Remember that time is precious for every coach, but, above all, for every player, at every level, so do not waste it. This doesn't mean that a coach should not run a 10-minute drill, but do not overabuse these lengthy drills. It is better to have six 5-minute drills than three or four 10-minute drills because:

- First, you avoid the boredom of a drill with the same repetitions for too long.
- Second, you can cover more varied fundamentals, with an higher intensity.

Is That All?

The following details are as important as the preceding aspects of a drill. You and your assistant coaches should follow these guidelines when running a drill.

Explain the Drill

Before running a drill, spend a few minutes to explain its purpose, what you expect from the drill, the proper execution, and the time required. This is a key to gaining the best results.

Avoid Interruptions

There should be no long interruptions between one drill and the next.

Avoid stopping a drill several times to explain it, because the players will lose their concentration and intensity.

Limit Corrections

You and your assistant coaches should not make too many corrections during a drill. Let the players know, in a few words, the corrections needed for a wrong move or fundamental, but don't give them too many things to think about.

If you overburden them with too many corrections, they may not be able to execute the drill properly or assimilate the correction. If you need to explain a correction in more detail, or if a player repeats the same mistake, take him aside to show him how to avoid the mistake, without stopping the flow of the drill.

Take Care of the Details

Basketball is a game of details: a missed shot or a wrong pass can be determined by an inch.

For example, if you run a shooting drill, concentrate on this fundamental, but don't forget to correct and take care of passing, as well as moving without the ball, since these fundamentals are equally important.

Encourage Enjoyment

Don't forget that basketball is a game, whether you coach a high school, college, or pro team, and that the players must also enjoy their practice. Add one or two drills that can be fun.

Even if a particular drill doesn't totally stick to your philosophy, it could help to break a demanding practice and release the pressure for a while.

Let's Talk About You

It's time to take a step back. Let's talk about you. Once the preceding aspects or suggestions become a part of your philosophy of choosing and running a drill, you need to evaluate your personal skills for gaining the best results from the drills that you have adopted and running a satisfactory and effective practice.

Practice Patience

Even if the world was created in seven days, you cannot pretend to create a player or an offense in two practices. Be patient: ask your players first to crawl, then to walk, run, and, finally, sprint at full speed.

Normally, the experienced, winning coach will tell you that to see improvement, you need to wait one or two months, using constant repetitions. So don't expect that one drill can solve your problem in a day, like a magic trick. Be patient.

Be Flexible

If you see that a drill is not working—the players are tired, they do not run the drill in the proper way, you need to stop the drill too many times to correct the players, or for any other reason—be flexible. Reduce the length, stop to run, or change that particular drill.

Do not run the drill at any cost, like a Marine sergeant, because it will not have the effect that you had in mind.

At the End . . .

Some of you may have become impatient after reading this first chapter. We talked of premises, suggestions, details, but now you are starving. You "smell" only the flavors of the "big meal." It means tens of drills to taste and try, so now you want to see the "menu" immediately and start to order. Fine, but always remember the previous notes and suggestions to avoid "indigestion." Do not "eat" too many drills; choose the "courses" carefully.

Too many "courses," that is, drills that are not suitable to your philosophy, can be detrimental to you and your team.

Now, finally, let's start.

2

Basic Footwork and Cuts Drills

Footwork is the foundation for a skilled basketball player, involving moves that he will use tens of times during a game. Cuts without the ball are one of the most important phases of the offensive game, because during a game a player spends more than three-quarters of his playing time on offense without the ball.

In this chapter, we will show some basic footwork and cuts drills. Don't underestimate these two fundamentals of the game, because many times they separate the good players from the great ones.

FOOTWORK DRILLS

TWO-LINE CHAIR DRILL

Aim

The aim of the two-line chair drill is to teach to the players how to master the five basic types of footwork without the ball.

Equipment

- 16 chairs (or less)

Personnel

- The entire team
- Two coaches

How to Run the Drill

Five feet away from the right and left sidelines, form a line of eight chairs, each at the same distance from the other. Two groups of players are set outside the baselines, one opposite the other, while two coaches stand in the middle of the court, with one following and correcting one group of players and the other in charge of the second group.

At the command of the coaches, the first player of each group starts to run, at the beginning at a slow pace, and then, when the player masters the footwork, at a higher speed. When the player reaches the first chair, he executes one of the following footwork moves, based on what the coach asked before the beginning of the drill, as shown in Figure 2.1:

- One-count stop
- Two-count stop
- Change of pace
- Change of pace and direction
- Spin

The player then repeats the same movement when he reaches the other chairs, ending the drill when he gets to the opposite baseline. The second player of each group starts the drill when the teammate in front of him reaches the mid-court line. Each player repeats the drill on the other line of chairs.

Details to Teach and Underline

It is important to note the words "teach" and "underline" in the heading of this paragraph. That is because a coach must first teach, but then he must also underline the details of a certain move or fundamental every time it is not executed properly.

The following are the common points to teach and, if necessary, to underline on all four moves:

- Bend the knees on all the footwork moves in order to have good balance and to move more quickly.
- Tell the player to go lower than the height of the chair.

Follow these guidelines for each single move:

One-Count Stop

Tell to the players not to jump, but, instead, to bend their knees. If the player jumps, he will lose a split second in air, while the "must" for each basketball fundamental is to make as few moves as possible, and in the quickest way.

Players must land on the floor with the heels first, and then with the forefeet for "braking" the forward movement.

Players must not lean forward so they don't lose balance, and their eyes must be positioned straight ahead, not to the floor, because it is the head's position that dictates the player's balance.

The arms and the hands must be flexed and at the chest level, ready to receive the ball.

Two-Count Stop

Guidelines are the same as for the one-count stop, with the only difference being that the

FIGURE 2.1

player lands on the floor first with one, and then with the other foot.

Change of Pace

Correct a common mistake made by many players: Tell them to make a couple of quiet and normal steps before changing the pace at the last second, when they are near each chair, not short and choppy ones. When they face a defender, moving like this is like a phone call to tell him: "Hey, I am now going to make a change of pace!"

On a change of pace, the player must make a straight and forward step and go down on one leg, bringing the weight of the body on the forefoot of the forward leg, at the same time, taking a big, aggressive stride forward with the other leg, but without losing balance. To help his body move forward quickly, he must also help the move by quickly swinging his arms forward.

After the chance of pace, tell the players to keep the same pace for a couple of steps, in order not to give the defender time to recover in a game situation.

Change of Pace and Direction

Again, ensure that players make no choppy and short steps before the change of pace and direction.

While changing direction, the player must make a straight, forward step, not a lateral one. He must also rotate the pivot foot in the new direction, an important detail that helps the whole body go forward, not laterally, in order to cut with a crisp angle in the next direction. The toes of the forward foot must be pointed straight, not laterally. If the player makes a lateral step and then a change of direction, he will be forced to make a longer stride to go in the new direction. It means covering a longer distance, giving the defender the chance to recover.

Tell to the players to pass very near to the chair when they change direction. In this way, they will not give the defender the chance to recover in a game situation.

The player, while passing near the chair, should also have his arm opposite the

11

forward leg, bent at a 45-degree angle. The bent arm will protect the ball when the player beats the defender by dribbling in a game.

Spin

The player must again, as in the change of pace and direction, point his forward foot straight, and not laterally.

Tell the players to start to spin, putting the forward leg "into" the chair and not away. In this way they will be able to "block out" the defender in a game.

The player should pivot on the forefoot of the forward foot, and, at the same time, bend his legs at chair level.

The non-pivot foot must be pointed toward the new direction: If it is pointed laterally, the body will go laterally.

The head should turn to the new direction before the spin, to see all the court and reverse back again if the defender recovers.

While spinning, the player should swing his arm hard and pivot his leg in order to move his body more quickly in the new direction.

The player must stay low for the movement and not rise up on his legs at the middle of the spin. This will decrease the speed of the spin.

FIRST-STEP BASIC DRILL

We would like to put particular emphasis on the first-step drills, because many times a coach does not work on this small but extremely important move that is basic for moving without the ball as well as with the ball.

Aim

The first-step basic drill teaches how to take a strong, aggressive first step to beat the defender. Players need to master this move until it becomes automatic, because it is absolutely basic for a basketball player.

Equipment

- 5 balls

Personnel

- The entire team
- A coach

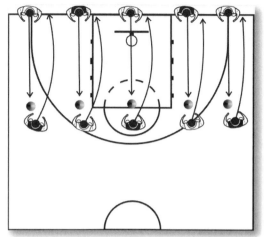

FIGURE 2.2

How to Run the Drill

Divide the team in two groups. One group is lined up off the court, along and behind the baseline, and the other one is at the free-throw-line extension. Each player in this latter group has a ball, which he holds with one hand at chest level. The players are paired. The coach stands behind the line of players at the baseline. The players at the baseline are positioned in the basic basketball position, with their knees flexed, their feet parallel, and their hands at chest level.

At the coach's command, the group with the balls drops them to the floor, and the other group of players at the baseline must catch the balls before they bounce twice on the floor, as shown in Figure 2.2. Then, the players exchange their positions.

The drill is repeated for a certain numbers of times. First, the players make the first step with the right foot for a certain numbers of times, and then with the left foot.

Details to Teach and Underline

- The most common mistake the players make is to step back with the same foot, before they step forward. This is a waste of time and moves.
- The players must "drop forward" with their body, at the same time, taking a strong, aggressive step, with head up and arms swinging forward, like runners at the start of a 100-meter race.
- The coach must stand behind the group of players at the baseline and correct them when they make the "extra" step back before the first-step.

13

FIRST-STEP AND DRIBBLE DRILL

Aim

The aim is the same as in the preceding drill, but with the ball.

Equipment

- 5 chairs
- 5 balls

Personnel

- The entire team
- A coach

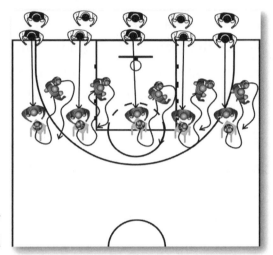

FIGURE 2.3

How to Run the Drill

The players are divided in five lines. They stand out of the court, along and behind the baseline, with a chair in front of each line and one ball on each chair. At the order of the coach, the first player in each line makes a hard and aggressive first-step, sprints, turns around the chair, makes a one-count stop fronting the basket, picks up the ball from the chair, and makes a strong, aggressive first dribble, going over the chair with the first dribble, as shown in Figure 2.3.

After a couple of dribbles, the player then quickly brings back the ball to the chair, and the second player in the line starts the drill. First, the players make the first dribble with the right hand for a certain numbers of times, and then with the left hand.

Details to Teach and Underline

- On the first dribble, the ball must hit the floor hard, in front and lateral to the forward foot, in order to get back quickly into the hand of the player, with the dribbling hand pushed as much as possible near the floor for better control of the ball.

- The player must make a change of pace on the dribble.

DROP-STEP AND DRIVE DRILL

Aim

The aim of this drill is to practice the first-step with the back to the basket and finish with a layup.

Equipment

- 4 balls

Personnel

- The entire team

FIGURE 2.4

How to Run the Drill

Divide the team into four groups, two be-hind the baseline, one on the left, and one on the right side of the half-court, with the other two groups, with two balls each, facing the baseline groups. At the command of the coach, the first players in the baseline groups run, catch the balls from their teammates, make a drop-step, then take an aggressive first-step and dribble to the basket, finishing with a layup, as shown in Figure 2.4.

Variation

The players start the drill from the mid-court line and execute the same pattern, but now front the basket, and make a different dribble, such as a direct, a cross-over, or a spin dribble (see Chapter 4, Dribbling Drills).

CUTS DRILLS

Players use cuts to get free and receive the ball, either to go straight to the bas-ket, play one-on-one, or start the offense. These moves are also used to get open

15

using a screen. Do not assume that a player will make these cuts automatically, but practice these moves as you normally practice any other fundamental. For example, if you run a passing or shooting drill, ask to the players to make a certain cut before receiving the ball for a shot or before receiving a pass. In short, include these cuts in any possible drill.

STATION DRILL

Aim

The aim of the station drill is to practice all four basic cuts.

Equipment

- 4 balls

Personnel

- The entire team

How to Run the Drill

Divide the team in four groups of three players each, with each group working in one half of each half-court. One passer with the ball is at the top of the lane, and one offensive player and one defensive player are at the wing spot. Call each group with a letter, as shown in Figure 2.5, and practice the specific moves, following this pattern:

- Group A: Front cut
- Group B: Backdoor cut
- Group C: V cut
- Group D: Reverse cut

The player starts the move, makes the re-

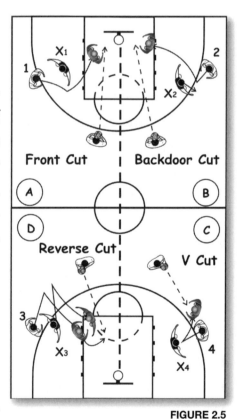

FIGURE 2.5

quested cut, receives the ball, and makes a layup without dribbling, while the defender simulates a certain defense (loose defense, overplay defense, etc.), moving slowly to facilitate the cut. After the shot, the shooter gets his own rebound, goes outside the lane, and becomes the passer, while the passer becomes the defender, and the defender becomes the offensive player, until all three players have performed the move.

Once all four groups end the drill, they move clockwise to the following spots for performing a different move: A goes to the B area, B goes to the C area, and D goes to the A area.

The coach decides how many of the same moves a player must perform or how long the drill must be run.

Once the players have mastered the cuts, the defenders will defend at 50 percent. Then the final step is to cover the offensive players at full speed and game conditions.

Details to Teach and Underline

- On all four cuts, the offensive player must start to move in a quiet and unassuming way, going in the opposite direction of where he wants to cut.
- Tell the player to take one or two normal steps before the cut; he should not "phone in" his move to the defender by making short, chopping steps.
- Tell the players not to watch the passer: this is another "alarm" signal to the defender.
- When the player is open and ready to receive the ball, he must present a target to the passer, that is, the hand farther from the defender.
- When the player makes a change of direction, he must rotate the foot that pushes the body in the new direction, pointing the toes in the new direction, in order to go laterally and not straight.
- Explain clearly to the players when to use a certain cut:
- Front cut: when the defender is below the offensive player
- Backdoor cut: when the defender is higher and aggressively overplaying

17

- V cut: if the defender does not allow the offensive player to make a front or backdoor cut
- Reverse cut: if the defense stops the cut inside the lane

Variation

The drill can also be run at different angles of the half-court, for example, in the corners and at the top of the lane.

FOUR LINES CUTS DRILL

Aim

The aim of the four lines cuts drill is to involve the entire team in a drill that requires all the players to move in the half-court and create a game situation.

Equipment
- 3 balls

Personnel
- The entire team

FIGURE 2.6

How to Run the Drill

Four groups are set, as shown in Figure 2.6: one at the top of the lane with the balls, two on the wings, and one under the basket, outside the baseline. Player 1 starts to dribble and then makes a reverse dribble or crossover dribble to the right side. As soon as 1 starts to dribble, 2 makes a backdoor cut (or a front or reverse cut, as indicated by the coach), receives the ball from 1, and makes a layup, with no dribble. Player 3 gets the ball and passes it to 4.

The players will rotate in this way: 2 goes to the end of 3 line, 3 goes to the end of 4 line, and 1 goes to the end of 2 line.

18

Details to Teach and Underline

- The ball handler must dribble at game speed.

- The cutter must make a crisp and angled cut, while also changing the pace.

- The cutter must present a clear target to the passer: the inside hand.

- The passer must make a good, strong pass, hitting the target given
  by the cutter.

- The cutter must not shoot a fancy layup, but instead use the backboard and protect
  the ball with the body and the other hand.

- The rebounder must make a good outlet pass if the shot is missed, or make a quick inbound pass if the shot is made: again, at speed and game conditions.

Variation

The coach can add two defenders: one on the ball handler 1 and one on the cutter 2. At the beginning, the defenders can play defense at 50 percent, and then play an aggressive defense in game conditions.

TWO-ON-TWO DRIBBLE AND CUT DRILL

Aim

The aim of the two-on-two dribble and cut is to teach the players to quickly read the situation on the court and react with the proper cut to the movement of the defense.

Equipment

- 4 balls

Personnel

- The entire team

How to Run the Drill

Form groups of four players, two players on offense and two on defense on both half-courts. At the beginning, the defense does not play aggressively, but simulates a certain type of defensive move, to which the offensive players react with the proper cut. Player 1, in the middle of the court, starts to dribble toward the basket and is guarded by X1, while 2 is on the right, in this case, wing spot, and guarded by X2. Based on how X2 simulates the defense on 2, this player will cut in front of X2 , or make a backdoor cut or a V cut.

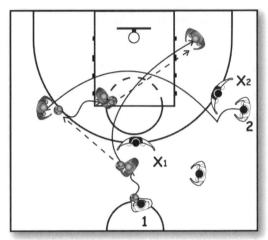

FIGURE 2.7

Player 2 cuts, receives the ball, and passes back to 1, who also made a cut (again, front, backdoor, or V cut) based on how X1 covers him, as shown in Figures 2.7 and 2.8. Once 1 has received the ball back, he starts the drill again. After a certain numbers of repetitions or a given time, the offensive players go on defense and vice versa.

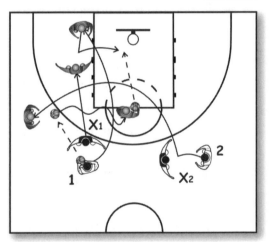

FIGURE 2.8

20

Details to Teach and Underline

- Tell the players to "prepare" the cut with one or two steps beforehand.
- The timing is basic: the two players must time the cuts and passing; it means not making a cut before the ball handler is ready to pass the ball.

Variation

Once the players have mastered the ability to read the defense and use the proper cuts, the defense plays aggressively.

3

Ball-Handling
Drills

An orange ball is the "tool" used on a basketball court. It can become a friend or one's worst enemy, if treated badly. Ball handling is the "elementary school" for a player, who needs to approach the ball gently to start the "feeling of this relationship," a relationship that should be positive and long-lasting.

DRILLS TO ADD TO PLAYERS' ROUTINES

Aside from the usual figure-eight circles around the body and other common ball-handling drills, we will suggest other drills to add to your players' ball-handling routine in this chapter.

DRIBBLES AT VARIOUS HEIGHTS DRILL

Aim

The aim of practicing dribbles at various heights is to begin the basic approach with the ball, as well as to improve the fingers' strength.

Equipment

- 1 ball per player

Personnel

- The entire team
- A coach

How to Run the Drill

The team is spread out on the half-court, with one ball for every player and the coach in front of the players, as shown in Figure 3.1. The players must pound the ball to the ground extremely hard, without losing the contact with the ball. The coach signals with one hand, changing the numbers of fingers, and the players must shout out the number he displays. This forces the players to dribble the ball without watching it.

They must dribble as fast as possible and with maximum power on each dribble, using the following dribbles:

Shoulder-height dribble: Pound the ball hard from shoulder height down to the floor, starting with the right hand, for 20 seconds. Repeat with the left hand, again for 20 seconds.

Hip-height dribble: Follow the same moves as the shoulder-height dribble, but now at hip height.

Knee-height dribble: Follow the same moves as the shoulder-height dribble, but at knee height.

Ankle-height dribble: Follow the same moves as the shoulder-height dribble, but at ankle height.

Details to Teach and Underline

- The players must pound the ball with the maximum power and at maximum speed.
- Even if players lose control of the ball at the beginning, by working at the

FIGURE 3.1

22

highest intensity, they will improve their ball handling, their speed at dribbling, and the strength in their fingers and hands.

- Players must be trained to watch, not the ball, but the hand of the coach instead.

SIDE AND LATERAL DRILL

Aim

The aim of practicing side and lateral dribbles is to begin the approach with the different types of dribbles, as well as to improve the fingers' strength.

Equipment

- 1 ball per player

Personnel

- The entire team
- A coach

How to Run the Drill.

The team's and coach's positions are the same as in the previous drill. The players should practice the following dribbles with each hand, always calling back the number of fingers raised by the coach:

Front change of hands: The players start to change hands in front, first, with the ball at hip level, then below knee level.

Front change of hands, touching the floor: While the players change hands, they must touch the floor with the non-dribbling hand.

Lateral dribble: The players dribble the ball laterally from outside the hip, first with the right hand and then with the left hand.

In-and-out dribble: The players make an in-and-out dribble, first with the right hand and then with the left hand.

Run the drill for 20 second with one hand and 20 seconds with the other hand.

23

Details to Teach and Underline

- On these drills, the players must dribble the ball below waist level.
- They must pound the ball hard and at top speed.
- They must not watch the ball, but instead call out the numbers of fingers raised by the coach.

Variation

When the players are skilled in these dribbles, they can make the same types of dribbles with two balls.

ONE-PLAYER TENNIS-BALL DRILL

Tennis-ball drills are excellent for improving ball handling. Using tennis-balls forces the player to pay attention to two moves and not focus only on the ball.

Aim

The aim of this drill is to boost ball-handling skill, increasing the difficulty as well as improving eye-hand coordination.

Equipment

- 1 ball per player
- 1 tennis ball per player

Personnel

- The entire team
- A coach

How to Run the Drill

The team is spread out in the half-court, facing the coach. Each player starts to dribble the basketball with the right hand, holding the tennis ball with the left hand, as shown in Figure 3.2. At the

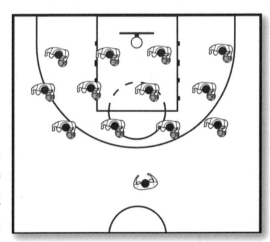

FIGURE 3.2

coach's command, the players throw the tennis ball up in the air, without stopping the dribble. Then they catch the tennis ball and switch hands, dribbling with the left hand and holding the tennis ball with the right hand. They run the drill for a certain numbers of repetitions, or for a set time.

Details to Teach and Underline

- Tell the players to keep knees bent while dribbling.
- They must pound the ball hard when dribbling.
- They must always look ahead, not at the basketball, while dribbling.

TWO-PLAYER TENNIS-BALL DRILL

Aim

The aim of the two-player tennis-ball drill is to boost ball-handling skill, but now increasing the difficulty by working with a teammate.

Equipment

- 1 ball per player
- 1 tennis ball per player

Personnel

- The entire team
- A coach

How to Run the Drill

Pair the players, with one basketball and one tennis ball per player. The two players, one in front of the other, start to dribble, one using the right hand and the other the left hand, each holding a tennis ball in the other hand, as shown in Figure 3.3.

FIGURE 3.3

As the coach shouts, "Toss," they throw the tennis balls to each other, yelling "High" or "Low" to indicate how to toss the ball, always without stopping the dribble. They repeat the drill, changing the dribbling hand.

Then, after a certain number of repetitions or a given time, at the command of the coach, they make a crossover dribble while tossing the ball to each other.

Variation

The drill is run in the same way, but now the players move randomly on the court.

4
Dribbling Drills

Chocolate is delicious, but if you eat too much, it is bad for your health. The same is true about dribbling, because if overdone by the players, it could be bad not only for them, but also for the "health" of the coach.

THE NEED FOR DRIBBLING DRILLS

It's important to learn how to use dribbling, and, above all, when to use one dribbling technique over another. In this chapter, we will introduce different dribbling drills that must be run at 50-percent speed by less-experienced players in order to master the technique and improve their speed, or at maximum speed for advanced players.

FOUR-CORNERS DRILL

Aim

The aim of the four-corners drill is to have the whole team working on the same dribbling drill to improve different types of dribbles.

Equipment

- 13 chairs
- 8 balls

Personnel

- The entire team

How to Run the Drill

Form four lines of three chairs each, starting from each corner of the half-court to the free-throw area, and set one chair in the middle of the free-throw area. The team is divided into four groups, each one set in a corner with two balls per line, as shown in Figure 4.1.

The first player of each line starts to dribble, going around the chairs using the type of dribble asked by the coach, such as:

- Between the legs
- Behind the back
- Crossover
- In-and-out
- Reverse
- Hockey dribble
- Change of pace
- Step back

Once the dribbler reaches the chair at the free-throw area, he makes a two-count stop and a reverse pivot, then passes the ball to the teammate on the line where he started the drill and goes at the end of the same line. The drill is run for a certain numbers of repetitions or a set time.

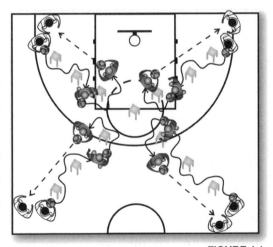

FIGURE 4.1

28

Details to Teach and Underline

- The players must start the drill in a basic basketball position, knees bent, with the ball between waist and chest, the wrist flexed.
- They must make a strong "first step" (see Chapter 1, Basic Footwork Drills) and dribble at chair level, with the head up.
- Players should pump the ball hard to the floor, acting as if they are in an actual game.

Variation

The player drives using one of the following advanced dribbles:

- Double between-the-leg
- Double crossover
- Double behind-the-back
- Step back and crossover (or between-the-legs, behind-the-back, or change of pace)

CALL-THE-SIDE DRILL

Aim

The aim of the call-the-side drill is to teach to the players to watch the basket and not the ball while dribbling, and also to shoot in the traffic.

Equipment

- 8 balls

Personnel

- The entire team
- Two coaches

How to Run the Drill

The team is divided into four groups, two on each half-court, outside of the baseline, with two balls per group. The coach is out of the court near the basket, outside the baseline.

At the command of the coach, the first two players in the line make a self-pass, tossing the ball outside the three-point line, then sprint to catch the ball, make a reverse, and dribble hard to the basket. While the players are dribbling to the basket, the coach raises one hand. If he raises the left hand, the players exchange the side of the court where they shoot: the right

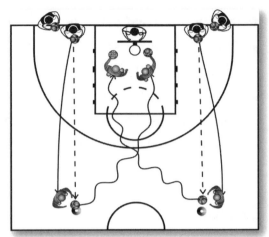

FIGURE 4.2

player on the left side, and the left player on the right side. If the coach raises the right hand, the players finish with a layup on the same side as they started to dribble to the basket, as shown in Figure 4.2. Both players must finish with the layup, without colliding with each other. The drill is run for a certain numbers of repetitions or a set time.

Details to Teach and Underline

- Dribble with the head up.
- Change the pace of the dribble while going to the basket.

Variation

Based on the coach's command, one player makes a jump shot and the other drives to the basket.

CALL-THE-NUMBERS DRILL

Aim

The aim of the call-the-numbers drill is to force the players to dribble without watching the ball.

Equipment

- 6 balls

Personnel

- The entire team
- Two coaches

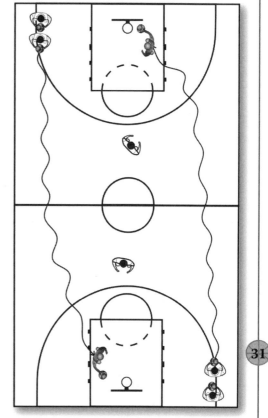

FIGURE 4.3

How to Run the Drill

The team is divided into two groups, one on the right side of a half-court, outside the baseline, and the other one on the right side of the other half-court, outside the baseline. There are three balls per group, and the two coaches are set near the mid-court line, facing the players.

At the coach's command, the first player of each line starts to speed-dribble toward the opposite basket, always watching the coach in front of him. At a certain point, the coach raises up one hand, displaying a number of fingers. The player must call the number of raised fingers, and then continue to speed-dribble and finish with a layup, as shown in Figure 4.3. Once he reaches the free-throw-line extension, he must go to the basket with no more than a dribble. The second player of each line starts the drill when the player in front of him has crossed the mid-court line.

Then the drill continues with the lines moving from the right side to the left side, so that the players now dribble with the left hand. The drill is run for a certain numbers of repetitions or a set time.

Details to Teach and Underline

- The first player to run the drill must pound-dribble, while waiting for the signal from the coach.

- When he starts the speed-dribble, he must make a strong first step, avoiding the extra step (see Chapter 1, Basic Footwork Drills).
- After the player in front of him has started the drill, the second player in the line pound-dribbles, with knees bent, waiting his turn to start the drill.

Variation

The coach can use different types of dribbles, such as a hockey-dribble, between-the-legs dribble, behind-the-back dribble, spin-dribble, in-and-out dribble, and so on.

EIGHT TYPES OF DRIBBLES DRILL

Aim

The aim of this drill is to teach different types of dribbles on the court to use under different game situations.

Note: This drill can be run when the players have mastered the basic dribbles and are ready to use advanced or combined dribbles. It involves two types of basic dribbles run at the same time.

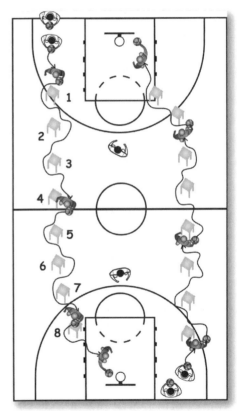

FIGURE 4.4

Equipment

- 16 chairs
- 6 balls

Personnel

- The entire team

How to Run the Drill

The players are divided into two groups, each one on the right side of the two half-courts, outside the baseline, with three balls per group. The groups have a line of eight chairs, from one baseline to the other one, in front of them.

At the coach's command, the first player of each group starts to dribble, using a different type of dribble when he faces each chair, as shown in Figure 4.4. The coach calls the following dribbles:

- First chair: doublecrossover
- Second chair: double between-the-legs
- Third chair: double behind-the-back
- Fourth chair: double in-and-out
- Fifth chair: in-and-out and behind-the-back
- Sixth chair: fake reverse
- Seventh chair: crossover and between-the-legs
- Eighth chair: step back and crossover

The second player in line starts the drill when the first one has crossed the mid-court line. The drill is run for a certain numbers of repetitions or a set time.

Details to Teach and Underline

- The players must make each type of dribble at 50 percent of their speed at the beginning, and then, when they have mastered the advanced dribbles, at full speed.
- When they go around the chair, they must "brush" the chair, that is, stay as close as possible to the chair without making a large cut around it. Players must become accustomed to this move so that when they face a defender, it will help them to beat him and prevent his recovering.
- On any type of dribble, players must change pace when they go around the chair.

Variation

The coach can later add standing defenders, instead of the chair. He can also ask the players to go under the dummy defenders' arms as they are extended at shoulder level, so they can get used to going down as much as possible while dribbling in order to beat a defender.

CHASER DRILL

Aim

The aim of the chaser drill is to teach players not to watch the ball, and to make fakes and change pace and direction while dribbling and when they are chased by the defenders.

Equipment

- 1 ball for every player

Personnel

- The entire team

How to Run the Drill

Each player has a ball, and the team is spread out in the half court. Designate a player to be the "chaser," and set him at the free-throw line, while the other players are set inside the court along the baseline.

At the coach's command, the players try to dribble toward the opposite basket, while the chaser tries to tag them, as shown in Figure 4.5.

Every time one player is tagged by the chaser, loses the control of the ball, or dribbles outside the court's lines, he becomes a chaser. All the chasers try to stop the remaining players from reaching the opposite basket. The drill ends when only one or two players have not become chasers.

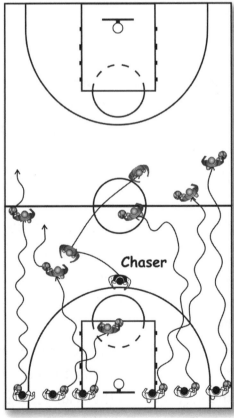

FIGURE 4.5

34

Details to Teach and Underline

- Remind the players not to watch the ball, and to make a crisp change of pace and direction to avoid becoming a chaser, as well as to fake with the head and the shoulders, not only with the ball, in order to beat the chaser.

Variation

To make the drill more difficult, you can add one or two chasers at the beginning of the drill.

IN-THE-LANE DRILL

Aim

The aim of the in-the-lane drill is to practice different types of dribbling in a small area, such as the lane.

Equipment

- 1 ball for every player

Personel

- The entire team

How to Run the Drill

The team is divided into two groups, set on each half-court, with one ball per player. The players form a line in the middle of the half-court. The first player speed-dribbles diagonally in the lane, and, when he touches the mid-sideline of the lane, he makes a cross-over dribble, going toward the oppo-

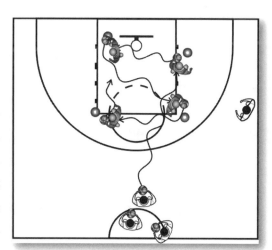

FIGURE 4.6

site. Here he makes a spin-dribble; when he reaches the opposite corner, he makes a through-the-legs dribble and goes to the other corner, where he makes a behind-the-back dribble and scores a layup, as shown in Figure 4.6. Then, he repeats the drill, starting from the left side. The drill is run for a certain numbers of repetitions or a set time.

Details to Teach and Underline

- As usual, never look the ball.
- Change pace on every dribble.

Variation

Ask the players to perform advanced and combination dribbles. Run the drill at full speed after the players have mastered the basic dribbles.

OUT-OF-TRAP DRIBBLING DRILL

Aim

The aim of the out-of-trap dribbling drill is to practice escaping from a trap.

Equipment

- 1 ball for every three players

Personnel

- The entire team

How to Run the Drill

The team is divided into groups of three players, with two defenders and one offensive player, who has the ball. The offensive players are set at the baseline, and the defenders are set outside the sidelines, one line on the left and the other on the right.

The drill starts with the first offensive player, 1, who steps on the court, under the basket. The two defenders, X1 and X2, step in and set themselves just outside the corners the three-second lane. At the command of the coach, the two defenders try to trap the dribbler. The dribbler has two options: make a dribble back to avoid the trap, or make a speed-dribble to split the trap, options based on the position of the defenders, as shown in Figure 4.7.

The drill ends when the dribbler is trapped or when he crosses the midcourt line. When one of these options happens, three other players step on the court and run the drill.

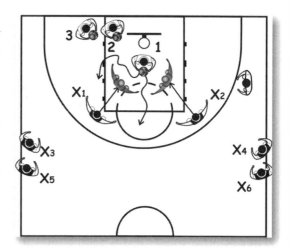

FIGURE 4.7

Details to Teach and Underline

- Always dribble with the head up in order to watch the court and the defenders' moves.
- Don't try to escape from the trap using a reverse dribble, because it is easier to trap.
- If the dribbler tries to split the trap, make a long speed-dribble, matched to a change of pace.

Variation

The drill can be run on the full court and ends when the dribbler drives to the basket and scores, or when he is trapped.

SPEED-DRIBBLE DRILL

Aim

The aim of the speed-dribble drill is to work on the speed-dribble, which is rarely taught and run in practice.

Equipment

- 1 ball per player
- 1 clock

37

Personnel

■ The entire team

How to Run the Drill

The team is divided into three groups. Each group forms a line, one in the middle of the court, and the other two near the left and right sidelines, with three balls per line. All three groups are aligned at the free-throw-line extension.

At the coach's command, the first three players speed-dribble from one free-throw-line extension to the other one and come back, as shown in Figure 4.8. They should make seven repetitions in 30 seconds or thirteen repetitions in 1 minute.

Details to Teach and Underline

■ Push the ball hard in front of and laterally to the same foot of the dribbling hand.

■ Watch the court instead of the ball.

Variation

The players dribble from baseline to baseline, making five repetitions in 30 seconds or eight repetitions in 1 minute.

Note: The number of repetitions depends on the ages and the conditioning level of the players.

THE TUNNEL DRILL
Aim

The aim of the tunnel drill is to teach players to drive hard to the basket, going straight to the rim.

FIGURE 4.8

Equipment

- 12 chairs
- 4 balls

Personnel

- The entire team
- Two coaches

How to Run the Drill

The team is divided into two groups, one on the left side and one on the right of the the half-court. Two parallel lines of three chairs, each chair four feet from the other, are set on the left and on the right sides of the half-court, as shown in Figure 4.9.

FIGURE 4.9

The first player on the right line has the ball, pound-dribbles, and is fronted by the coach, who pushes and holds him for few seconds. Then, the coach lets the player drive to the basket. The player goes to the basket with no more than two dribbles, finishing with a layup. The player on the right side of the half-court starts the drill first, followed by the player on the left side. After the layup, they get the rebound and go to the other line. The drill ends after a certain number of repetitions or after a set amount of time.

Details to Teach and Underline

- While the coach is pushing hard, the player must keep his knees bent so he maintains balance, protects the ball, and is ready to explode to the basket.
- Do not make more than two dribbles to the basket; also, change the pace.

Variation

The player makes a jab-step before driving hard to the basket. The coach stands near the basket, at the end of the line of the chairs, and fouls the player who is finishing with a layup.

THREE-CHAIR DRILL

Aim

The aim of the three-chair drill is to add difficulty to driving to the basket.

Equipment

- 3 chairs
- 4 balls

Personnel

- The entire team

How to Run the Drill

The team is divided into two groups, each one lined up in the middle of the half-court. Set three chairs on in the middle lane of the half-court, as shown in Figure 4.10.

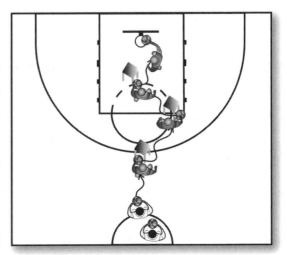

The first player dribbles toward the first chair and makes a crossover dribble. Then, when he approches the second chair, he makes a behind-the-back dribble, and, finally, when he reaches the third chair, he makes a between-the-legs dribble before exploding to the basket, finishing with a layup.

FIGURE 4.10

After a certain number of repetitions per player or a set time, the last two chairs are moved to the opposite side, so the players can practice with the other hand.

Details to Teach and Underline

- Start the drill by making pound-dribbles, before dribbling hard to the first chair.
- Always change pace while executing the three different types of dribbles.
- Always keep knees bent while dribbling.

Variation

Use different types of dribbles, such as in-and-out, reverse, step-back, or advanced dribbles (see Eight Types of Dribbles Drill earlier in this chapter).

5

Shooting Drills

As important as footwork, passing, dribbling, and playing one-on-one may be, the ultimate target of this game called basketball is to have the ball pass through the rim. If you do not shoot, and shoot with a good percentage, it's very difficult to win a game. In the last ten years, basketball has become more physical; the players are bigger and more aggressive on defense. Scoring a layup or a jump shot is a tough job, so players must be able to shoot under pressure and with physical contact.

For these reasons, and, also, perhaps, because not enough time is spent on teaching the mechanics of shooting or players do not make enough repetitions, the shooting percentages have decreased at every level in the past years.

Therefore, shooting is arguably the most important of all the drills we cover in this book. In this chapter, we will provide you with numerous shooting drills, including some that we believe are different and innovative.

SHOOTING-DRILL TIPS

Here are some tips on shooting drills:

- Run drills using the shots that the players will need in the game and from the spots you want the players to shoot from, based on the game speed.
- The drills must be more intense and difficult than in the game.
- Keep a record of each player's missed and made shots in the jump-shooting drill, so that both you and the players can have actual data on which to base their improvement in this fundamental.

LAYUP DRILLS
CATCH-AND-DRIVE DRILL
Aim

The aim of the catch-and-drive drill is to teach the players to bend their legs, using the opposing arm to protect the ball, and shoot a layup with no more than one dribble.

Equipment

- 4 balls
- 2 chairs

Personnel

- The entire team
- Two coaches

How to Run the Drill

Divide the team into two groups, one in each half-court. Place a chair at the right corner of the free-throw line on both half-courts, with one ball on each chair. One player with another ball, 2, is near the chair, and the rest of each group lines up outside the three-point line. One coach, with his back to the basket and a ball, stands to the left of the chair, with his arms extended at shoulder level.

The first player of the group, 1, fakes a cut to the left, then runs to the right side of the chair. He changes the pace and the direction, and, once he is in front of the chair, makes a one-count stop, bending his knees at chair level. He picks up the ball, swings the ball below knee level, makes a strong and aggressive first step and, simultaneously, a hard pound-dribble, going under the extended arms of the coach, and scores a layup, without dribbling more than once, as shown in Figure 5.1. After the layup, 1 recovers his ball and goes near the chair.

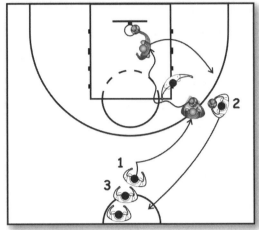

FIGURE 5.1

Player 2, who holds another ball, puts it on the chair, and runs to the end of the line in the middle of the court. Player 3 starts to move and runs the same pattern as 1.

The drill is repeated on the left side of the half-court, and it ends after a certain numbers of repetitions or after a set amount of time.

Details to Teach and Underline
- Don't jump on the one-count stop, but keep knees bent.
- Use the nondribbling arm, bent at a 45-degree, angle, to protect the ball.
- Watch the basket, not the ball, on the dribble.
- Make a strong, long step, matched with a hard dribble, landing with the forward foot and with the ball touching the floor beyond the coach's hip.

Variation
The coach can also ask to the players to make any of the following:
- Behind-the-back dribble
- Between-the legs-dribble
- Reverse dribble
- In-and-out dribble.

REVERSE, CATCH, AND DRIVE DRILL

Aim

The aim of the reverse, catch, and drive drill is to teach footwork, to move without the ball, and to drive to the basket.

Equipment

- 2 balls
- 8 chairs

Personnel

- The entire team
- Two coaches

How to Run the Drill

Divide the team into two groups, each group in the middle of each half-court. Set two chairs at each corner of the free-throw area on both half-courts, as shown in Figure 5.2, with one ball on each chair. The player starts to run, and, at the coach's command, left or right, he fakes to go in one direction, and then goes in the opposte direction in between the two chairs, makes a reverse, then picks up the ball on the chair and drives to the basket, finishing with a layup.

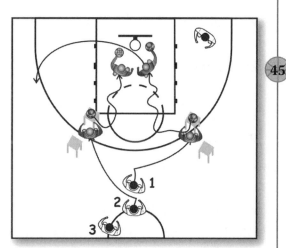

FIGURE 5.2

Then the next player repeats the same move on the other side of the court. The coach or a teammate retrieves the balls and sets them on the chairs for the next player.

Each player runs the drill for a certain numbers of repetitions or for after a set amount of time.

Details to Teach and Underline

- Change pace and direction before going in between the chairs.
- Bend the knees when picking up the ball from the chair.
- Make a straight drive to the basket, not a curve.

Variation

The player can make a different type of dribble to drive to the basket, such as behind-the-back, between-the-legs, or crossover.

CATCH, DROP-STEP, AND DRIVE DRILL

Aim

The aim of the catch, drop-step, and drive drill is to teach footwork, to move without the ball, and to drive to the basket.

Equipment

- 4 balls
- 4 chairs

Personnel

- The entire team

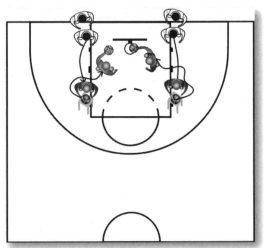

FIGURE 5.3

How to Run the Drill

Divide the team into four groups, two at each half-court, at the baseline. Set two chairs, a ball on each chair, a couple of feet from the corners of the free-throw area.

The first player on the right line runs to the chair, makes a one-count stop, picks up the ball, makes a drop-step, and drives to the basket, with no more than one dribble. He finishes with a layup, as shown in Figure 5.3.

The player recovers the ball and puts it on the chair, and then the player on the left line makes the same move. After shooting, they go to the end of the other line. Run the drill for a certain numbers of repetitions or for a set amount of time.

Details to Teach and Underline

- Bend the knees when picking up the ball from the chair.
- Make a quick, strong, and aggressive first-step and dribble to finish to the basket.
- Make a straight drive to the basket, not a curve.

Variation

The players of both groups start the drill at the same time, both driving to the basket. In this case, they will also work on shooting in traffic.

SELF-PASS, SWEEP, AND DRIVE DRILL

Aim

47

The aim of the self-pass, sweep, and drive drill is to teach footwork, to move without the ball, and to drive to the basket.

Equipment

- 12 balls
- 4 chairs

Personnel

- The entire team

How to Run the Drill

Divide the team into four groups, two in each of the half-courts on the wing spots, with one chair in front of each line. The first three players in each line have a ball.

The first player on the right line makes a self-pass, with the ball bouncing in front of the chair. Then he runs, makes a one-count stop, picks up the ball, sweeps it across and below the knees, and makes a strong, aggressive first-step and long dribble, finishing with a layup. No more than one dribble is permitted when going to the basket.

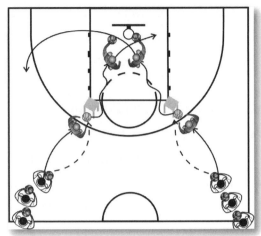

FIGURE 5.4

He then recovers the ball, passes to the player on the left side, and goes to the end of the left line, as shown in Figure 5.4. The first player in the left line makes the same move and, then, alternatively, all the other players on the right and left sides. The drill is run for a certain number of repetitions or for after a set amount of time.

Details to Teach and Underline

- Bend the knees on the one-count stop.
- Quickly bring the ball to the side of the body, in between the hip and the chest.
- Make an aggressive and very quick sweep of the ball.
- Make a strong and aggressive first step and dribble, pushing the ball hard to the floor on the forward foot's side.

Variations

The players make different dribbles (behind-the-back, between-the-legs, crossover, in-and out, or hockey dribble), before driving to the basket.

They can also run the drill at the same time. In this case, they will also work on shooting in traffic.

CATCH, DRIVE, AND CROSSOVER DRILL

Aim

The aim of the catch, drive, and crossover drill is to teach footwork, to move without the ball, and to drive to the basket.

Equipment

- 4 balls
- 6 chairs

Personnel

- The entire team

How to Run the Drill

Divide the team into four groups, two in each of the half-courts on the wing spot, with one chair in front of each line, a ball on the chair, and one chair in the middle of the free-throw area. The first player on the right side of the court runs toward the chair, makes a one-count stop, picks up the ball, drives toward the chair in the middle of the free-throw area, makes a cross-

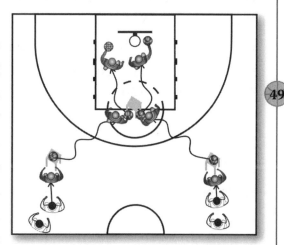

FIGURE 5.5

over dribble, and drives to the basket, finishing with a layup after no more than one dribble, as shown in Figure 5.5. The drill is run for a certain number of repetitions per player or for a set amount of time.

Details to Teach and Underline

- Bend the knees on the one-count stop.
- Quickly bring the ball to the side of the body, in between the hip and the chest.

- Make an aggressive and very quick sweep of the ball.
- Make a strong and aggressive first step and dribble, pushing the ball hard to the floor on the side of the forward foot.

Variations

The players make different dribbles (behind-the-back, between-the-legs, cross-over, in-and-out, hockey dribble), before driving to the basket.

They can also run the drill at the same time. In this case, they will also work on shooting in traffic.

TWO-BALL PASS AND DRIVE DRILL

Aim

The aim of the two-ball pass and drive drill is to teach players to dribble, pass, and shoot in more difficult situations than the game condition, as well as to co-ordinate two different moves without watching the ball when driving.

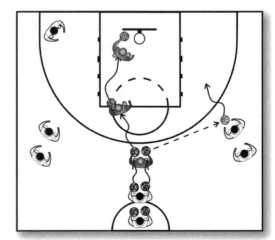

FIGURE 5.6

Equipment

- 6 balls

Personnel

- The entire team
- A coach

How to Run the Drill

Divide the team into three groups, one group with the balls in the middle of the half-court, about 6 feet outside of the three-point line, the second one on the right, and the third on the left-wing spots. Each of the first three players in the middle line has two balls. A coach is set in the corner.

The first player in the middle line starts to pound-dribble and, at the coach's command, makes a speed-dribble. When he reaches the three-point line, he makes a one-hand push pass to the player to the left, then drives to the basket with the other ball, finishing with a layup, after no more than one dribble, as shown in Figure 5.6. The shooter gets his own rebound, and the three players rotate clockwise.

After a certain number of repetitions or after a set amount of time, they pass to the right and drive to the basket to the left.

Details to Teach and Underline
- Pound-dribble the ball hard.
- Always watch the basket, not the ball or the receiver.
- Make a crisp and hard pass to the player in the wing.
- Change pace while finishing with a layup shot.

Variation
The set is the same, but the players with two balls in the middle line now make a one-hand push pass to the left side, and then a one-hand push pass to the right side, in order to cut to the basket and receive the ball back from the passer on the right side, finishing with a layup, without dribbling. Then they do the opposite, receiving the ball back from the passer on the left side.

SLIDE, RUN BACKWARD, SPRINT, AND SHOOT DRILL
Aim
The aim of the slide, run backward, sprint, and shoot drill is to shoot lay-ups when fatigued.

Equipment
- 1 ball

Personnel
- The entire team

How to Run the Drill

Divide the team into two groups, one group under a basket facing the mid-court line, and one in the middle of the court. The first two players of this group have one ball each, while one player is set in the lane and acts as a rebounder. At the coach's command, the first player in the line under the basket slides to the corner to his right. When he touches the sideline, he turns, runs backward until he reaches the hash mark, then sprints diagonally to the basket, receives the ball from the first player of the group in the middle of the court, and finishes with a layup without dribbling.

Then, he repeats the same move on the other side of the half-court, as shown in Figure 5.7, while the rebounder in the lane passes the ball back to the next player in the group in the middle of the court. The second player in the line under the basket starts the drill when the first player, who began the drill, starts to sprint diagonally to the basket. Then, the players rotate in this way: the shooter goes to the end of the passer's line, the passer becomes the rebounder, and the rebounder goes to the end of the shooter's line.

Each player runs the drill for a certain number of repetitions, or for after a set amount of time.

Details to Teach and Underline

- Make a diagonal, not large cut, when sprinting toward the basket.
- Continually emphasize that the receiver of the pass must ask for the ball, presenting his outside hand as a target to the passer.

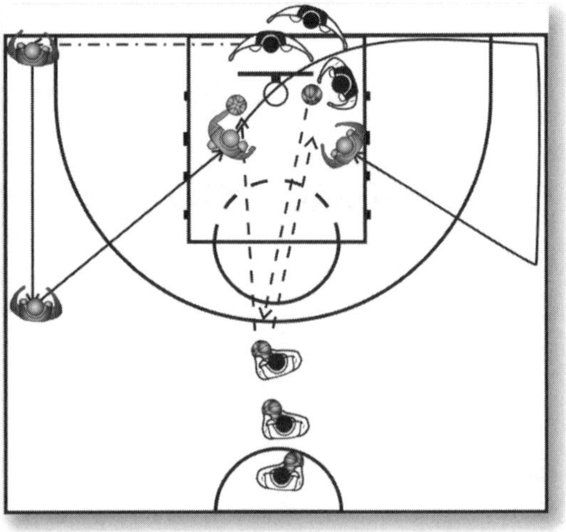

FIGURE 5.7

Variation

The rebounder touches or pushes the player who is shooting the layup with a foam pad to make the drill tougher.

Divide the team into two groups and run the drill in the two half-courts as a competition: the first group that scores a certain number of baskets first (or scores more baskets after a given amount of time) wins.

BACK-TO-THE-CORNER DRILL

Aim

The aim of the back-to-the-corner drill is to teach players to move without the ball, pass, cut, and shoot a layup.

Equipment

- 4 balls

Personnel

- The entire team

How to Run the Drill

Divide the team into four groups, two groups on one half-court and two groups on the other half-court. One group is under the basket and the other is in the middle of the half-court, outside the three-point line, with two balls for each group.

The player under the basket passes the ball to the player in the middle of the court, goes outside in the right corner, and receives the ball back. Then, he cuts in the three-second lane, receives the ball, and finishes with a layup.

He recovers the ball, passes it again to the player in the middle of the half-court, and repeats the same move on the other side of the court, as shown in Figure 5.8.

After he finishes the drill, he goes to

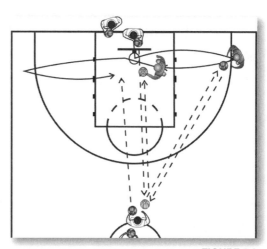

FIGURE 5.8

53

the end of the middle line, while the player in the middle line goes to the end of the line in the corner. Each player runs the same pattern ten times, five times on the right side and then five times on the left.

Details to Teach and Underline
- All the cuts must be angled and matched with a change of pace.
- The cutter must not watch the passer until he is in the corner.

Variation
The drill is run in the same way, but the players shoot a reverse layup.

JUMP-SHOT DRILLS

The jump shot is a basic fundamental that every player, whether he plays on the perimeter or inside the lane, must master. Don't be afraid to spend a lot of time

on the jump-shot drills, particularly on those that require constant focus, with the challenges of time, the contest against himself, or against a teammate.

Note: We will show drills on mid-range jump shooting, but, practically, all the drills can also be run to practice the three-point shot. You can also add a defender to these drills, who defends at the beginning at 50 percent on the shooter.

SEATED-ON-THE-CHAIR DRILL

Aim
The aim of the seated-on-the-chair drill is to teach the proper mechanics of the jump shot.

Equipment
- 10 chairs
- 10 balls

Personnel
- The entire team

How to Run the Drill

Place five chairs in a semicircle around each basket and inside the three-second lane, as shown in Figure 5.9. The players are seated on the chairs, with the ball held only with one hand. Starting from the first chair on the left, each player shoots, without standing up, as shown in Figure 5.9.

After the player on the last chair has shot, every player moves to the next chair in a clockwise rotation. The drill ends when the player seated on the first chair on the left shoots from the fifth chair.

The players should make a complete routine, shooting from first to fifth chair, three times.

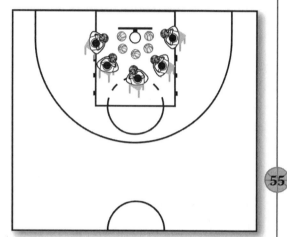

FIGURE 5.9

Details to Teach and Underline

- The player must align the ball, the hand, and the elbow, with the ball resting on the fingers of the hand, not in the palm.
- He must block the arm and not bring the arm down while shooting the ball.
- He must extend the arm going up, not forward, with the index finger of the hand pointed toward the middle of the basket.
- At the end of the shot, the hand must be completely open, not pointing down to the floor.

Variations

After the players have mastered the proper technique of release and follow-through of the ball, ask them to shoot, again with one hand only, standing, without jumping. Then, add the nonshooting hand to the ball.

Then, move the players farther from the basket and have them shoot, without

55

jumping, and, finally, when their technique is perfect, ask them to make a jump shot, always starting near the basket and gradually increasing the distance from the basket. Finally, ask them to make self-pass, catch the ball, and make a jump shot.

REVERSE DRILL

Aim

The aim of the reverse drill is to practice footwork and shooting.

Equipment

- 4 chairs
- 4 balls

Personnel

- The entire team

56

How to Run the Drill

Divide the team into two groups, with each group lined up in the middle of a half-court. Set two chairs at the corners of the free-throw area, a ball on each chair, and two rebounders under the basket.

The first player runs toward the left chair, makes a reverse, picks up the ball, and shoots without dribbling. Then, he repeats the same moves on the right side of the court, as shown in Figure 5.10.

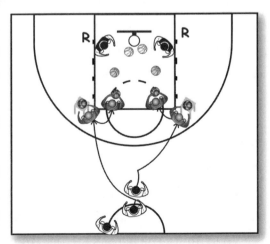

The two rebounders get the balls and put them on the chairs.

The shooters become rebounders and the rebounders go to the end of the line. The drill ends after a certain number of shots or after a set amount of time.

FIGURE 5.10

Details to Teach and Underline

- The player stays low when he reaches the chair.
- Players should end the reverse by pointing their feet toward the basket.

Variation

The players change pace and direction before shooting, then a dribble, a shot fake, or a shot fake and a dribble, after the reverse.

The same player shoots twice in a row, once from the right, and then from the left corner of the free-throw line.

DROP-STEP DRILL

Aim

The aim of the drop-step drill is to practice shooting fundamentals and footwork.

Equipment

- 4 chairs
- 4 balls

Personnel

- The entire team

How to Run the Drill

Divide the team into four groups, two in the two corners of each half-court. Two chairs are set at the corners of each free-throw area, with a ball on each chair and two rebounders under the basket.

The first two players of each groups, as shown in Figure 5.11, run toward the

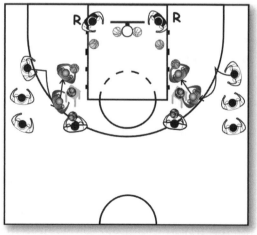

FIGURE 5.11

chair, pick up the balls, make a drop-step, and shoot without dribbling.

The two players under the basket get the rebounds and put the balls back on the chairs. The shooters become rebounders, and the rebounders go to the end of the opposite line from where they started the drill. The drill ends after a certain number of shots or after a set amount of time.

Details to Teach and Underline

- Stay low while reaching the chair.
- End the drop step by pointing the feet toward the basket.

Variation

The players make a dribble, a shot fake, or a shot fake and a dribble after the drop-step.

TWO-CHAIR, TWO-BALL DRILL

Aim

The aim of the two-chair, two-ball drill is to practice shooting fundamentals and footwork.

Equipment

- 4 chairs
- 4 balls

Personnel

- The entire team

How to Run the Drill

Divide the team into two groups, one in each half-court and outside the baseline. Set two chairs at the corners of the free-throw area, with one ball

FIGURE 5.12

on each chair, and two rebounders in each three-second lane.

The first player runs to the chair, circles around, catches the ball on the first chair, makes a two-count stop, and makes a jump shot. Then, he runs in the three-second lane, comes out, circles around the other chair, and makes another jump shot, as shown in Figure 5.12. The drill ends after a certain number of shots or after a set amount of time.

Details to Teach and Underline
- Keep knees bent on the two-count stop before shooting.

Variation
The players dribble and make a shot fake, or a shot fake and a dribble before shooting.

TURN, DRIBBLE, AND SHOOT DRILL
Aim
The aim of the turn, dribble, and shoot drill is to work on shooting and footwork.

Equipment
- 4 chairs
- 4 balls

Personnel
- The entire team
- Two coaches

How to Run the Drill
Divide the team into two groups. In each half-court, set two chairs, three feet from each other, at the free-throw line. Each group is set outside the three-point line, with the first player of the group facing the mid-court line. The coach, with the ball, stands near the mid-court line, facing the player.

The coach passes the ball to the first player, and, at the same time, tells him to turn right or left. The player turns, dribbles hard to the lane, stops in between the two chairs, and makes a jump shot, as shown in Figure 5.13. The drill ends after a certain number of shots or after a set amount of time.

Details to Teach and Underline

- Stay low on the two-count stop before shooting.
- Make a hard-bounce dribble when pulling up the ball for the shot.

Variation

The players make a shot fake or a shot fake and a dribble before shooting.

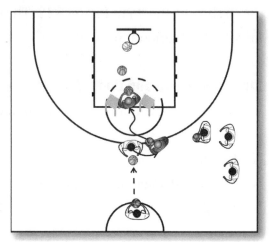

FIGURE 5.13

60

M DRILL

Aim

The aim of the M drill is to work on shooting on the run.

Equipment

- 6 chairs
- 4 balls

Personnel

- The entire team

How to Run the Drill

Divide the team into two groups. In each half-court, place two chairs near the mid-court line about 20 feet apart and one chair in the middle of the half-court, near the free-throw line arc.

The first player is in the left corner, outside the three-point line, while two rebounders, with one ball each, are inside the three-second lane. The rebounder on his left side passes the ball to the player, who has stepped inside the three-point arc, and now shoots.

After the shot, the player runs around the chair near the mid-court, reaches the corner of the free-throw area, receives the ball, and shoots. Then, he circles around the chair in the middle of the half-court, stops at the other corner of the free-throw lane, receives the ball, and shoots. Finally, he runs around the other chair at the mid-court line, goes in the corner, receives the ball, and shoots, as shown in Figure 5.14. The drill ends after a certain amount of repetitions per player.

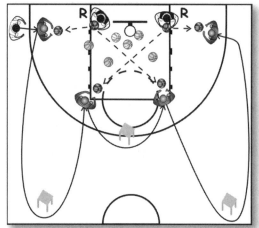

FIGURE 5.14

61

Details to Teach and Underline
- Run on all phases of the drill.
- S tay low on the two-count stop before shooting.

Variation
The player can make a dribble, a shot fake, or a shot fake and a dribble before each shot.

X DRILL
Aim
The aim of the X drill is to work on shooting that has been affected by fatigue.

Equipment
- 6 chairs
- 4 balls

Personnel

- The entire team

How to Run the Drill

Divide the team into two groups. In each half-court, set two chairs near the mid-court line about 15 feet apart and one chair in the middle of the half-court, near the three-point arc. The player is in the left corner of the free-throw area, while two rebounders, with one ball each, are inside the three-second lane. The rebounder on the left side passes the ball to the player, who shoots. After the shot, the player runs around the chair near the mid-court line and the chair in the middle of the court, reaches the other corner of the free-throw area, receives the ball, and shoots.

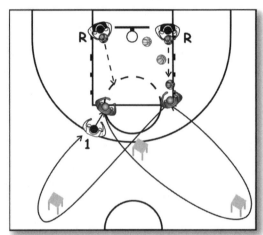

FIGURE 5.15

He then repeats the pattern for a total of four shots, as shown in Figure 5.15. The drill ends after a certain amount of repetitions per player.

Details to Teach and Underline

- Run on all the phases of the drill.
- Stay low on the two-count stop, before shooting.

Variation

The player can make a dribble, a shot fake, or a shot fake and a dribble before each shot.

FOUR-CHAIR DRILL

Aim

The aim of the four-chair drill is to teach players to use a screen, to cut to get in position to receive the ball, and to take a jump shot on the move. The player must shoot on the run.

Equipment

- 4 chairs
- 4 balls

Personnel

- The entire team

How to Run the Drill

Divide the team into groups of three player each. Four chairs, with one ball on each chair, are set at the four corners of the three-second lane, two near the baseline and two at the corners of the free-throw area. Two rebounders are in the lane.

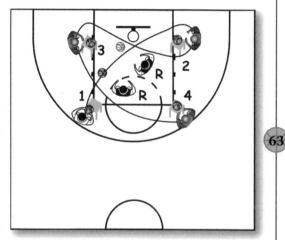

FIGURE 5.16

The first player starts the drill at about three feet away and in front of chair 2 at the right side of the half-court near the sideline, as shown in Figure 5.16. He makes a strong, aggressive fake to the right, then cuts in the lane, curls around chair 1 at the left corner of the free-throw area, catches the ball, and takes a jumper. Then, he cuts back in the lane, curls around chair 2 on the right near the baseline, and shoots. He then cuts again in the lane, curls around chair 3, catches the ball, and shoots. He ends the drill by cutting diagonally in the lane, curling around chair 4 at the right corner of the free-throw area, and shooting.

The rebounders get the balls and put them back on the chairs. The drill ends after a certain amount of repetitions per player.

Details to Teach and Underline

- Change the pace while approaching the chairs.
- Point the feet toward the basket when picking up the ball.

Variations

- Advanced version: The player must complete the drill within a certain amount of time.
- The drill can also be run as a competition among all the players on the team, with a coach who counts and records the made and missed shots.

AROUND-THE-WORLD DRILL

Aim

The aim of the around-the-world drill is to work on shooting on the run.

Equipment

64

- 6 chairs
- 4 balls

Personnel

- The entire team

How to Run the Drill

Divide the team into groups of three players, with one group per half-court. Set two chairs on the two low-post areas near the three-second lane, and one inside the free-throw area; position two rebounders, with one ball each, in the lane. The player starts the drill on the left side, near the baseline, at the left of the chair, as shown in Figure 5.17. He

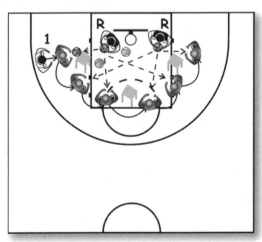

FIGURE 5.17

receives the ball, shoots, circles around the first chair, receives again, and shoots. Then, he repeats the same pattern with the other two chairs, for a total of six shots. The drill can be repeated more than one time per player.

Details to Teach and Underline
- Always stay low on the knees when receiving the ball.
- Always point the feet toward the basket.

Variation
The player makes a dribble, a shot fake, or a shot fake and a dribble before shooting.

THREE-LINE DRILL

Aim
The aim of the three-line drill is to practice different footwork, finishing with jump shots.

Equipment
- 6 balls
- 3 chairs

Personnel
- The entire team
- Three coaches

How to Run the Drill
Divide the team into three groups, one on the right side of the half-court, the second one near the sideline on the left side of the half-court, and the third one on the wing spot on the left side. Each group has two balls. One chair is placed 2 feet outside the right corner the free-throw area, a second chair in the middle of the free-throw area, and the third one in the short corner of the left side of the half-court,

65

while one coach stands near each chair. The drill is shown in Figure 5.18.

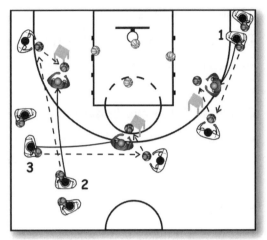

FIGURE 5.18

Player 1 passes the ball to the coach, who puts the ball on the chair. Then 1 runs to the chair, makes a one-count stop, picks up the ball from the chair, makes a drop step, and drives to the basket, finishing with a jump shot.

Player 2 makes the same moves, but, when he picks up the ball from the chair, makes a reverse step, finishing with a jump shot.

Player 3 makes the same moves, but, when he picks up the ball from the chair, makes a crossover step, finishing with a jump shot.

Player 1 goes at the end of 2's line, 2 to 3's line, and 3 to 1's line. The drill is run for a certain number of shots per player or after a set amount of time. The drill is repeated on the other side of the floor.

Details to Teach and Underline
- Stay low on the knees when receiving the ball.
- Always point the feet toward the basket.

Variation
The players make a different type of dribble (behind-the-back, between-the-legs, in-and out, hockey dribble) before driving to the basket.

TWO-BALL, TWO-SHOT DRILL
Aim
The aim of the two-ball, two-shot drill is to practice ball handling, passing, and shooting skills in a difficult drill.

66

Equipment

- 1 chair
- 6 balls

Personnel

- The entire team
- Two coaches

How to Run the Drill

The team is lined up in the middle of the half-court, with the first three players with two balls each. Two coaches stand, one on the left wing and one on the right; one chair is set in front of the line of the players.

The first player starts to pound-dribble. After few seconds, he dribbles toward the chair and, when facing it, makes a one-hand push pass to the right, drives with the other ball to the left of the chair, and makes a jumper. Then, he circles the chair on the side, receives the ball back, and makes another jump shot, as shown in Figure 5.19.

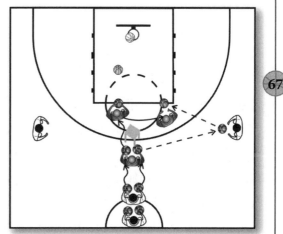

FIGURE 5.19

The drill is run for a certain number of shots per player or after a set amount of time.

Details to Teach and Outline

- Stay low on the knees throughout the drill.
- Make a strong one-hand push pass, using the chest of the receiver as a target.

Variation

Change the position of the line of the players and/or add a different dribble be-

67

fore shooting, such as behind-the-back, between-the-legs, crossover, in-and-out, and so on.

CHANGE-OF -PACE-AND-DIRECTION DRILL

Aim

The aim of the change-of-pace-and-direction drill is to practice footwork, ball handling, and shooting skills.

Equipment

- 4 chairs
- 4 balls

Personnel

- The entire team
- Two coaches

How to Run the Drill

The team is divided into two groups, one on the left and one on the right side of the half-court, with a chair in front of each group, and one ball on each chair. One coach, holding a ball, is near each chair, and two other chairs are set at each corner of the free-throw area. The first two players of each group sprint toward the chair, pick up the ball, sweep it, and dribble hard toward the other chair, as

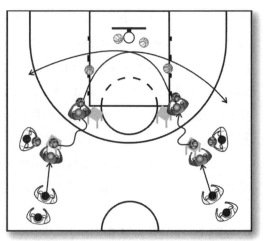

FIGURE 5.20

shown in Figure 5.20. When they reach the chair, they make a crossover dribble, changing the pace and direction, then, after a two-count stop, make a jump shot, when they reach the other chair. The drill is run for a certain number of shots per player or after a set amount of time.

Details to Teach and Underline

- When picking up the ball, make a hard, aggressive, quick sweep of the ball, going under the knees.
- On the change of pace and direction, while making the crossover, point the feet toward the basket.

Variation

The player makes a type of dribble other than the crossover.

TWO-SHOOTER DRILL

Aim

The aim of the two-shooter drill is to practice passing and shooting under difficult conditions.

Equipment

- 1 chair
- 6 balls

Personnel

- The entire team

How to Run the Drill

The team is divided into two groups, one lined up in the wing spot of the half-court, with a chair in front. The first three players have two balls each, while the other group is in the corner. A coach is in the opposite corner

The first player in the wing starts to pound-dribble, then, after a few seconds, dribbles toward the chair and,

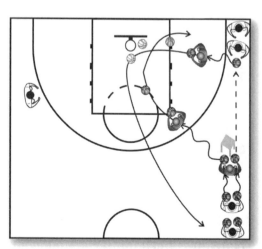

FIGURE 5.21

when facing it, makes a one-hand push pass to one player in the corner, who makes a jump shot (or a drive), based on the coach's command. Then, he drives to the opposite side of the pass and makes a jumper (or a drive to the basket), as shown in Figure 5.21. The drill is run for a certain number of shots per player or after a set amount of time. The drill is repeated on the other side of the floor.

Details to Teach and Outline

- Stay low on the knees throughout the drill.
- Make a strong one-hand push pass, using the receiver's chest as the target.

Variation

Change the positions of the two groups of players and add a different dribble before passing and shooting, such as behind-the-back, between-the-legs, crossover, and so on.

PASS-AND-SHOOT DRILL

Aim

The aim of the pass-and-shoot drill is to practice passing and shooting under difficult conditions.

Equipment

- 1 chair
- 4 balls

Personnel

- The entire team

How to Run the Drill

The team is lined up in the middle of the half-court, with a chair placed in the the free-throw area. Each player has one ball. Two players stand on the left and right wings, the player on the right wing with a ball.

The first player in line starts to pound-dribble, then, after a few seconds, dribbles toward the chair and, when facing it, makes a one-hand push pass to the player in the left wing, receives the ball from the player on his right, and makes a jump shot, as shown in Figure 5.22. After a certain number of shots per player or a set amount of time, a pass is made to the player on the right wing, and the ball is received from the player on the left wing.

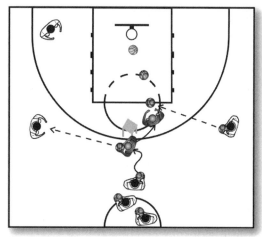

FIGURE 5.22

Details to Teach and Outline

- Stay low on the knees throughout the drill.
- Make a strong one-hand push pass, with the chest of the receiver as the target.

Variation

The player adds a specific dribble before passing, such as behind-the-back, between-the-legs, crossover, and so on.

THREE-MAN, TWO-BALL DRILL

Aim

The aim of the three-man, two-ball drill is to practice the jump shot, always shooting from a different position and on the run.

Equipment

- 4 balls

Personnel

- The entire team

71

How to Run the Drill

Divide the team into groups of three players, each group with two balls. The drill is run on both half-courts. The drill starts with two players, each one with a ball, set outside the three-second lane, and one player under the basket. The two outside players shoot and then run for the rebounds, while the inside player runs out of the lane, receives, and shoots, and so on, as shown in Figure 5.23.

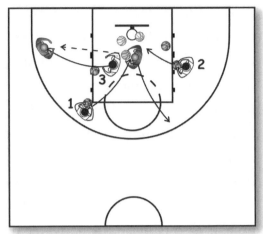

FIGURE 5.23

The players must continually shoot, rebound, pass, and move outside the three-second lane. The drill ends after a specified number of shots, made shots, or set amount of time. Then, another group of three players runs the drill.

Details to Teach and Underline

- Run, but do not rush, and always be in control before shooting.
- Avoid wasted motion.
- Get ready to shoot before receiving the ball, and not after.
- Make the first shot and go to the rebound in two separate motions.

Variation

The drill can be competitive: the first player, who makes a certain number of shots, wins, and the others do sprints.

MACHINE-GUN DRILL

Aim

The aim of the machine-gun drill is to practice the jump shot on the run.

Equipment

- 2 balls

Personnel

- The entire team

How to Run the Drill

Divide the team in groups of three players, with one ball per group. The drill is run on both half-courts. One shooter is on the right wing outside the three-second lane, one passer with the ball is outside the three-point line, and one rebounder is near the basket. The passer makes a couple of hard dribbles to the left side of the court, then makes a crossover dribble (or another type of dribble), changes direction, and passes to the shooter on the wing (who, in the meantime, has made a V step before receiving the ball). The shooter shots the ball and goes under the basket, and, if the shot is missed, the rebounder gets the ball, and shoots under the basket.

In the meantime, moving clockwise, the passer replaces the shooter, the shooter becomes the rebounder, and the rebounder becomes the passer, as shown in Figure 5.24.

The drill can be run for a certain number of shots, made shots, or for a given amount of time.

FIGURE 5.24

Details to Teach and Underline

- Run, but do not rush, and always be in control.
- Avoid wasted motion.
- Get ready to shoot before receiving the ball and not after.
- After the first shot, go to the rebound in two separate motions.

73

Variations

The drill can be competitive if a coach counts the made shots of each player. The first one who scores a specified number of shots, wins.

POINT-SHOT DRILL

Aim

The aim of the point-shot drill is to practice shooting from different spots on the floor.

Equipment

- 14 cones

Personnel

- The entire team

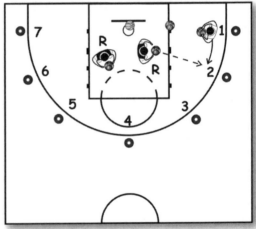

FIGURE 5.25

How to Run the Drill

74

The team is divided into groups of three players, and the drill is run on both half-courts. Mark seven spots inside the three-point arc with cones, chairs, or tape, as shown in Figure 5.25. Two rebounders stand inside the three-second lane with two balls, while the shooter stands on spot 1. He receives the ball and shoots right away: if he makes the shot, he runs to spot 2 and shoots, and so on until he reaches spot 7.

   If he misses a shot, he must shoot from that spot until he makes it. The drill is run twice, first from right to left and then from left to right.

Details to Teach and Underline

- The shooter must be ready to shoot (with the hands, the body, and the legs), before receiving the ball.

- While setting up to shoot to another spot, he must always have his feet pointed toward the basket.

Variation

The player makes a specified dribble before shooting.

55-SECOND DRILL

Aim

The aim of the 55-second drill is to practice shooting and to put pressure on the shooter.

Equipment

- 4 balls
- 2 watches

Personnel

- The entire team
- Two coaches

How to Run the Drill

The team is divided into groups of three players, one shooter with the ball, one rebounder inside the lane, and one passer with another ball. The drill is run on both half-courts. A coach stands outside the three-point line on each half-court with a watch. At the coach's command, the shooter shoots and moves to another spot, receives the second ball from the passer, and so on for 55 seconds, as shown in Figure 5.26.

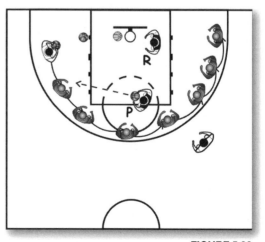

FIGURE 5.26

75

The shooter cannot shoot twice from the same spot, but, instead, must move to another spot. The passer must move 10 to 15 feet away from the shooter.

A manager or another player records the missed and made shots over a 55-second period. Then the players have 5 seconds to change roles: the shooter becomes the rebounder, the passer becomes the shooter, and the rebounder becomes the passer. After all three players in this group have performed the drill, another group steps in.

Details to Teach and Underline

- The shooter must assume the shooting position for the entire drill, that is, be ready to shoot before shooting and not after receiving the ball.
- Stress the importance of always pointing the feet toward the basket.
- Use the same form and mechanics until the last shot.

Variation

The player makes a specified dribble before shooting. The drill can also become a contest among the three players of each group, or of one group versus the other groups. The winner is the player or the group with the most made shots.

FULL-COURT SHOOTING AND DRIBBLING DRILL

AIM

The aim of the full-court shooting and dribbling drill is to practice shooting and dribbling, working full court at top speed.

Equipment

- 12 chairs or cones
- 12 balls

Personnel

- The entire team

How to Run the Drill

The team is divided into four groups of three or four players each, set at four corners of the court, with three balls for each group. Two passers stand at the corners of the free-throw area on both half-courts, and six chairs or cones are placed along and near the sideline of the court, as shown in Figure 5.27.

At the same time, the first player of each group passes the ball to the passer, and then, after faking a cut in the opposite direction from the point he passed the ball, goes toward the ball and makes the move and shot ordered by the passer. The following is a list of the possible shots:

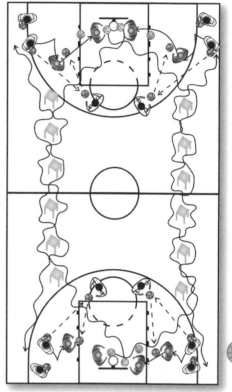

FIGURE 5.27

- Catch and jump shot
- Shot fake, dribble, and jump shot
- Step-back dribble and jump shot
- Any other type of dribble and jump shot

After the shot, the player gets his own rebound and dribbles at full speed around the chairs or cones until he reaches the other half-court and goes to the end of the line on that corner.

The drill is run for a certain number of made shots or after a set amount of time.

Details to Teach and Underline

- Make a hard fake before receiving the ball.

- Go low on the knee and get ready to shoot immediately before receiving the ball, not after.
- Do not watch the ball while dribbling at full speed.

FIVE-PLAYER SHOOTING DRILL

Aim

The aim of the five-player shooting drill is to practice passing and shooting, involving five players at the same time.

Equipment

- 6 balls

Personnel

- The entire team

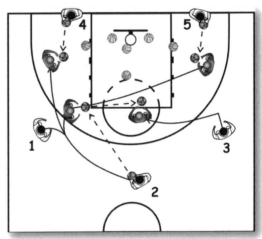

FIGURE 5.28a

How to Run the Drill

Divide the team into two groups of five players each, with one group in each half-court. Players 4 and 5, with one ball each, stand outside the baseline, one on the left and the other on the right side, while 1 and 3 are on the left- and right-wing spots, and 2, with the ball, is in the middle of the half-court. Player 1 fakes a cut to the the ball, then changes direction and pace and receives the ball from 2.

At the same time, 3 fakes a cut and then runs at the free-throw line, receives the ball from 1, and makes a jump shot.

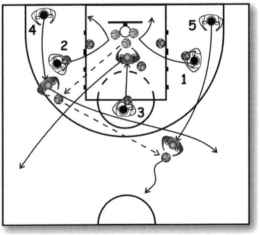

FIGURE 5.28b

78

After the pass to 1, 2 cuts toward 4, receives the ball, and makes a jump shot. Player 1, after the pass to 3, cuts toward 5, receives the ball, and makes a jump shot, as shown in Figure 5.28a.

After the shot, 1, 2, and 3 get their own rebounds, while 4 and 5 enter the court. Player 3 passes to 4, and 4 passes to 5, who dribbles to the center of the half-court. Players 1 and 2 replace, respectively, 4 and 5, and the drill goes on, as in Figure 5.28b. The drill ends after a certain number of shots or after a set amount of time.

Details to Teach and Underline
- Stress the importance of the passes to the shooters.
- Shooters' feet must always point toward the basket.

NINE-PLAYER CONTINUOUS DRILL
Aim

The aim of the nine-player continuous drill is to practice shooting and work on conditioning.

Equipment
- 6 balls
- 3 stopwatches

Personnel
- The entire team
- 3 coaches or managers

How to Run the Drill
The team is divided into three groups of three players each. Three coaches, each one with a stopwatch, are set outside the baseline at mid-court. Three players stand at the baseline: 1 is in the left corner, 2 under the basket, and 3 in the right corner. All three players have a ball and face, respectively, 4, 5, and 6, who stand

on the mid-court line.

On the other half-court, along the baseline, 7, 8, and 9 each have a ball. Players 4, 5, and 6 run toward the basket at the same time. Players 4 and 6 cut to the basket at the free-line-extension, then receive the ball from 1 and 3, respectively, and shoot, while 5 stops at the free-throw line, receives from 2, and shoots.

After shooting, 4, 5, and 6 get their own rebounds and replace passers 1, 2, and 3, who, after the passes, run to the opposite basket and repeat the same pattern. The drill ends after a certain number of shots in a set amount of time. Here some examples:

- 80 shots in 4 minutes
- 100 shots in 5 minutes
- 120 shots in 6 minutes

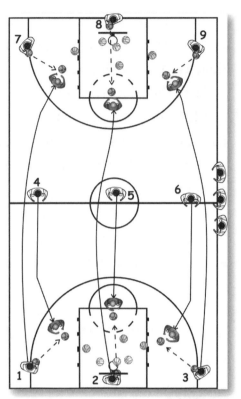

FIGURE 5.29

The coaches must keep a record of the missed and made shots in a set amount of time.

Details to Teach and Underline

- Stress the importance of making an accurate pass to the shooters.
- The shooters must be ready to shoot before receiving the ball, not after.

Variation

Before shooting, the players make a specific type of dribble. In this case, the number of shots can be decreased.

REACH-THE-FIVE DRILL

Aim

The aim of the reach-the-five drill is to practice dribbling and shooting under pressure.

Equipment

- 4 balls

Personnel

- The entire team

How to Run the Drill

Divide the team into two groups of six players each, who work on each half-court. Two shooters, each with a ball, are 10 feet away from the mid-court line, facing the opposite basket. One passer is on the left- and one is on the right-wing spot, and two re-bounders are under the basket. The two shooters speed-dribble; then, after they have crossed the mid-court line, pass to the passers. After faking a cut in the opposite direction, they cut toward the ball, receive it, and make a jump shot.

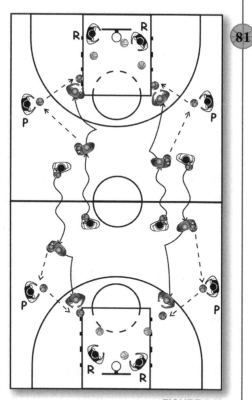

After the shot, they run back to the the point they started the drill and repeat the pattern, as shown in Figure 5.30. The shooter who scores the first five shots wins, and the loser does ten push-ups or sprints.

Details to Teach and Underline

- Stress the importance of moving without the ball and making angled cuts.

FIGURE 5.30

Variation

Before passing the ball to the passer, or when they receive the ball back, the players make a different type of dribble before shooting (crossover, between-the-legs, etc.).

SUPER-SIXTY DRILL

Aim

The aim of the super-sixty drill is to practice shooting on the run and under the pressure.

Equipment

- 4 balls

Personnel

- The entire team

How to Run the Drill

Divide the team into two groups of six players, each one set in the two half-courts. Three shooters with two balls are inside the three-point line, while three rebounders are inside the three-second lane. Each squad competes against the other. The players start to shoot and must make sixty made shots in 5 minutes, as shown in Figure 5.31.

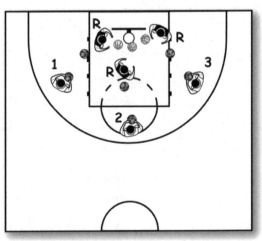

FIGURE 5.31

After five or ten made shots, the shooter becomes a rebounder and vice versa. The squad that loses does push-ups or sprints.

Details to Teach and Underline

- Stay low on the knees from the first to the last shot.

- Be ready to shoot before receiving the ball, not after.
- Always have the feet pointed toward the basket.

Variation

The player can make a specific type of dribble before shooting. In this case, decrease the numbers of made shots.

FIRST-TO-TWENTY DRILL

Aim

The aim of the first-to-twenty drill is to practice shooting under pressure.

Equipment

- 6 balls

Personnel

- The entire team

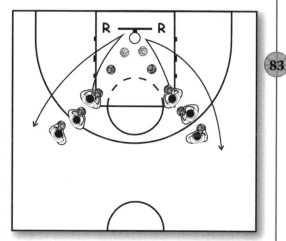

FIGURE 5.32

How to Run the Drill

Divide the team into four groups of three players, each one with three balls, two groups on one half-court and two on the other half-court, set on the left- and right-wing spots. The players shoot, get their own rebounds, and go to the end of their line, as shown in Figure 5.32. The group who scores the first twenty shots wins, and the losers do push-ups or sprints.

Details to Teach and Underline

- Stay low on the knees from the first to the last shot.
- Be immediately ready to shoot.
- Always have the feet pointed toward the basket.

Variation

The players make a specific type of dribble before shooting.

EIGHTY-SHOTS DRILL

Aim

The aim of the eighty-shots drill is to practice shooting on the run and under pressure.

Equipment

- 6 balls
- 1 stopwatch

Personnel

- The entire team

How to Run the Drill

Divide the team into two groups of six players each, set in the left- and right-wing spots of a half-court. Six players, each with a ball, are on the right side and six without the ball are on the left side, as shown in Figure 5.33.

One player without a ball fakes to cut away from the ball, then runs at the free-throw line, receives the ball, makes a jump shot, gets his own rebound, and goes to the passer's line, while the passer goes to the shooter's line. The group must make eighty shots in 7 minutes. If they do not reach the target, they must do push-ups or sprints.

Details to Teach and Underline

- Stay low on the knees from the first to the last shot.

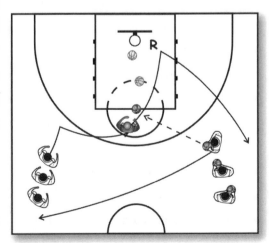

FIGURE 5.33

- Be ready to shoot before receiving the ball, not after.
- Always have the feet pointed toward the basket.

Variation

The players make a specific type of dribble before shooting. In this case, allow the players more time to end the drill.

BEAT KOBE BRYANT DRILL
Aim

The aim of the beat Kobe Bryant drill is to practice shooting and to challenge the players to concentrate on every shot.

Equipment
- 2 balls

Personnel
- The entire team

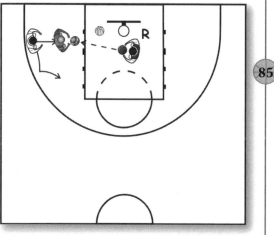

How to Run the Drill

The entire team is divided in twos, one shooter and one rebounder. The drill is run on both half-courts. The shooter is set outside the three-second lane and the

FIGURE 5.34

rebounder is inside. The shooter shoots continually, moving around the lane, and the rebounder passes the ball to him. If the shooter makes the basket, he gets one point; if he misses, "Kobe Bryant" gets two points, as shown in Figure 5.34.

The rebounder keeps the scoring record, and the shooter beats "Kobe Bryant" if he reaches ten points before "Kobe." Then, the rebounder becomes the shooter.

Details to Teach and Underline
- Stay low on the knees from the first to the last shot.

85

- Be ready to shoot before receiving the ball, not after.
- Always have the feet pointed toward the basket.

Variation

The player makes a specific type of dribble before shooting.

FREE-THROW DRILLS

Perhaps more than any other team sport, basketball is a mental game. It is important for a player to be focused every second he is on the court. When a player is at the free-throw line, without any opponent in front of him, with the chance to score one, two, or three easy points, he must be totally focused, without feeling the pressure of the crowd or need to make the free-throws.

This seems an easy job, but the mechanics of making this type of pressure shot must be accurately practiced, because many wins or losses depend on scoring the free-throws.

MADE-OR-RUN DRILL

Aim

The aim of the made-or-run drill is to practice free-throw shooting and put pressure on the shooter.

Equipment

- 2 balls

Personnel

- The entire team
- Two coaches

How to Run the Drill

Divide the team into two groups, each on a basket, lined up at the free-throw line, with two balls. Each player shoots two free-throws, gets his own rebounds, and passes the ball to the next teammate. Each group must score almost 70 percent of the free-throws. For every missed shot, each group makes one full-court sprint at the end of the drill, as shown in Figure 5.35.

One coach on each half-court keeps records of the missed and made free-throws.

Details to Teach and Underline

- Never rush; always wait a couple of seconds between one shot and the following one.
- Breath deeply before each free-throw, and make a couple of dribbles.
- Always watch the basket, not just during the seconds before shooting.
- Stay low on the knees and start the free-throw with the ball at eye level, not at or below the chest.

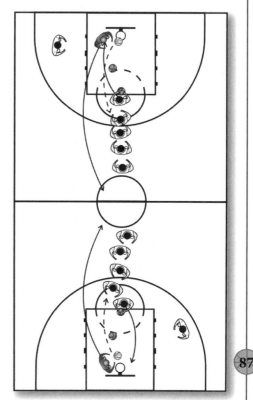

FIGURE 5.35

- Make the movement smoothly, simultaneously using the legs and the arms.
- Don't take a step back near the end of the free-throw (a big mistake), but instead stand at the free-throw line until the free-throw is made or the ball touches the basket.

TEN FREE-THROWS IN A ROW DRILL

Aim

The aim of the ten free-throws in a row drill is to practice free-throw shooting under pressure.

Equipment

- 4 balls

87

Personnel

- The entire team
- Two coaches

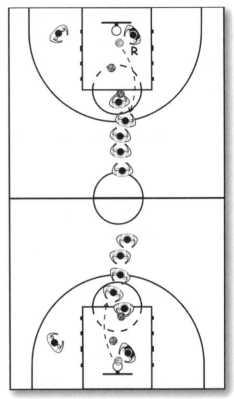

FIGURE 5.36

How to Run the Drill

This drill is run at the end of the practice. It puts a lot of mental pressure on the players when they shoot free-throws when they are very tired, the same conditions that they will face in a game.

Divide the team into two groups, each one at a half-court, with two balls and one rebounder in the lane. One coach stands outside the perimeter and keeps record of the missed and made free-throws. Each player must make ten free-throws in a row, and, if he misses one, he must go to the end of the line and repeat the routine a second time, as shown in Figure 5.36.

If he also misses the second attempt at shooting ten in a row, he must make as many full- or half-court sprints as he missed free-throws in the two sessions.

Details to Teach and Underline

- Never rush; always wait a couple of seconds between one shot and the following one.
- Breath deeply before each free-throw, and make a couple of dribbles.
- Always watch the basket, not just during the seconds before shooting.
- Stay low on the knees and start the free-throw with the ball at eye level, not at or below the chest.
- Make the movement smoothly, simultaneously using the legs and the arms.

- Don't take a step back near the end of the free-throw (a big mistake), but instead stand at the free-throw line until the free-throw is made or the ball touches the basket.

Variation

The two groups compete against each other.

ONE-PLUS-ONE-TO-TWENTY DRILL

Aim

The aim of the one-plus-one-to-twenty drill is to practice shooting free-throws under pressure.

Equipment

- 4 balls

Personnel

- The entire team
- Two coaches

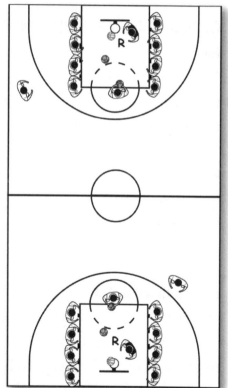

How to Run the Drill

Divide the team into two groups. Each group is aligned around the three-second lanes, on both half-courts, with one free-throw shooter and a rebounder under the basket and a coach on the perimeter, as shown in Figure 5.37.

Every player shoots one free-throw; if he makes it, he shoots another one, but if he misses the free-throw, the entire team rotates

FIGURE 5.37

and another player goes to the free-throw line for a one-plus-one. The first of the two groups that scores twenty free-throws wins, and the losers do sprints or push-ups.

Details to Teach and Underline

- Never rush, but instead wait a couple of seconds between one shot and the following one.
- Breath deeply before each free-throw, and make a couple of dribbles.
- Always watch the basket, not just during the seconds before shooting.
- Stay low on the knees and start the free-throw with the ball at the eye level, not at or below the chest.
- Make the movement smoothly, simultaneously using the legs and the arms.
- Don't take a step back near the end of the free -throw, but instead stand at the free-throw line until the free-throw is made or the ball touches the basket.

CLOSED-EYES FREE-THROW DRILL

Aim

The aim of the closed-eyes free-throw drill is to improve free-throw shooting accuracy using mental visualization.

Equipment

- 2 balls

Personnel

- The entire team

How to Run the Drill

The drill is run on both half-courts. Each player starts to shoot a certain number of free throws, using the proper technique and without rushing. The other players stand around the three-second lane and clap their hands to distract the shooter, as shown in Figure 5.38.

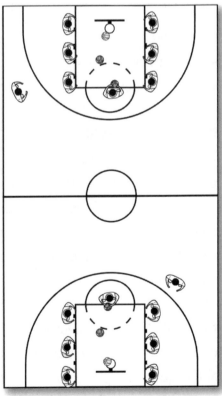

FIGURE 5.38

As soon as the shooter makes a specific number of free throws, he shoots the same number of free throws with his eyes closed, following the same routine and using the same mechanics as when he shot with his eyes open. The player must mentally visualize the movement and the ball entering the basket.

Details to Teach and Underline

- Never rush, but instead wait a couple of seconds between one shot and the following one.
- Breath deeply before each free-throw.
- Always watch the basket, not just during the seconds before shooting.
- Stay low on the knees and start the free throw with the ball at the eye level, not at or below the chest.
- Make the movement smoothly, simultaneously using the legs and the arms.
- Don't take a step back near the end of the free-throw, but stand at the free-throw line until the free-throw is made or the ball has touched the basket.

91

6

Passing Drills

*P*assing is the first and preferred word of any coach's vocabulary. This fundamental evokes in a coach the notes of a rhapsody; it is an aspect of the game that brings a coach to a state of peace. If basketball could be played without hearing the beats of the dribbles, it could be the dream game.

Moving the ball with a pass is quicker than moving it with a dribble. Making a skip pass can offer a better and a more open shooting solution. Getting the ball inside can create a higher-percentage shot. But, similar to shooting, passing is becoming a lost art.

Everybody is able to learn to pass, whether it is a two-hand or a one-hand push, an outlet, or other pass, but it is not as easy to know when and where to pass, or how to pass away from the defender.

Therefore, this fundamental must be carefully practiced and continually praised during every practice, and all the details must be taught and underlined, just as we advocate doing for all the drills in this book.

BEAT-THE-PASSER DRILL

Aim

The aim of the beat-the-passer drill is to teach to the players to fake before passing, and to work on different types of passes.

Equipment

- 1 ball for every three players

Personnel

- The entire team

How to Run the Drill

The team is divided into groups of three players, two on offense, with one ball, and one on defense, set in the central lane of the court. The two offensive players face each other 10 feet apart, while the defender is set in between the two offensive players.

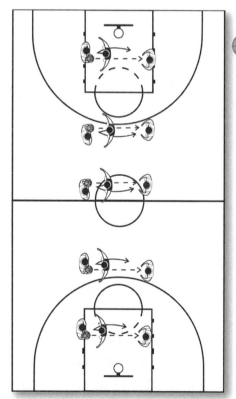

The two offensive players pass each other the ball, while the defender tries to "beat the passer." This means to touch or steal the ball, as shown in Figure 6.1. The offensive players can only make one step laterally, forward or back, without committing a traveling violation.

Every time the ball is stolen or touched by the defender, or if the passer does not pass in 3 seconds or makes a wrong pass to the receiver, the passer becomes the defender and the defender becomes the passer. The drill is run for 3 or 4 minutes. The offensive players are not permitted to make lob passes.

FIGURE 6.1

Details to Teach and Underline

- Before passing, fake using the head, the eyes, or the ball.
- Fake high before making a bounce pass, or fake down, before making a straight pass.
- "Read the passing lanes," that is, pass where the defender cannot steal or touch the ball, for example, near the head or the shoulder if the arm is down, or under the armpit, if the arm is high.
- Do not make a pass while jumping.
- The receiver must give a target to the passer: one hand or two hands.
- The receiver must go toward the ball.
- The defender must use defensive fakes, as well as wave his arms.

Variation

The distance between the two offensive players can be decreased to improve the difficulty of the drill.

94

"TRAPPERS" AND "GOALKEEPER" DRILL

Aim

The aim of the "trappers" and "goalkeeper" drill is to improve the players' passing under game conditions.

Equipment

- 1 ball

Personnel

- A minimum of ten players

How to Run the Drill

Divide the team into two groups, seven offensive players and three defenders, set in one half-court, while the rest of the team works on the other half-court on a different drill or fundamentals.

The seven players on offense form about a 15-foot circle. The three defenders are inside the circle: two "trappers" double-team, and the third is the "goalkeeper."

The players on offense pass each other the ball, following one rule: they cannot pass to the teammates on their left and right sides, as shown in Figure 6.2. The offensive player with the ball can only make one step laterally, forward or back, and the other teammates must stand in the same positions.

FIGURE 6.2

The trappers and the goalkeeper must try to deflect, touch, or steal the ball. If the defense is successful, the passer and the two teammates on his left and right side become the defenders. The drill is run for 3 or 5 minutes.

95

Details to Teach and Underline

- Before passing, fake, using the head, the eyes, or the ball.
- Fake high before making a bounce pass, or fake down, before making a straight pass.
- "Read the passing lanes," that is, pass where the defender cannot steal or touch the ball, for example, near the head or the shoulder if the arm is down, or under the armpit if the arm is high.
- Do not make a pass while jumping.
- The receiver must give a target to the passer: one hand or two hands.
- The receiver must go toward the ball.
- The defenders must use defensive fakes, as well as wave their arms.

Variation

Decrease the offensive players' circle to create a more difficult drill.

FOUR PASSERS–THREE DEFENDERS DRILL

AIM

The aim of the four passers–three defenders drill is to practice passing under game conditions in a restricted area, such as in the lane.

Equipment

- 1 ball

Personnel

- A minimum of seven players

How to Run the Drill

Set four offensive players, with one ball, at the four corners of the three-second lane, and three defenders inside the lane.

The players on offense pass the ball among themselves, standing in the same position, and are allowed to make only one step laterally, forward, or back while passing or receiving, without committing a traveling violation, as shown in Figure 6.3. If the ball is touched, deflected, or stolen, the passer and the teammates on his left and right become defenders, and the defenders go on offense. After four passes, the offensive player who receives the ball shoots. If he makes the shot, the defense stay in; if he misses, the offense goes on defense, and vice versa. The drill is run for 3 or 5 minutes.

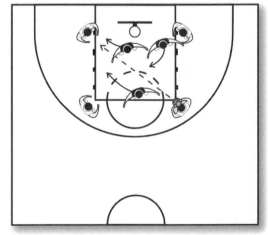

Details to Teach and Underline

- Fake using the head, the eyes, the shoulders, or the ball, before passing.
- Fake high before making a bounce pass, or fake down before making a straight pass.

FIGURE 6.3

- "Read the passing lanes," that is, pass where the defender cannot steal or touch the ball, for example, near the head or the shoulder if the arm is down, or under the armpit, if the arm is high.
- Do not make a pass while jumping.
- The receiver must give a target to the passer: one hand or two hands.
- The receiver must go toward the ball.
- The defenders must use defensive fakes, as well as wave their arms.

FIVE-PLAYERS STAR DRILL

Aim

The aim of the five-players star drill is to work on improving passing and passing speed.

Equipment

- 1 ball for every five players.

Personnel

- The entire team

How to Run the Drill

Divide the team into groups of five players each, with one ball per group. The players are set to form the points of a star, as shown in Figure 6.4.

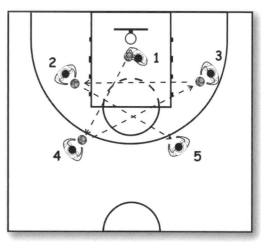

If the ball is in the hands of player 1, he passes the ball to the second player on his right (or the second player on his left), in this case, 4. Then 4 will pass to the second player on his right, 3, who will pass the ball to 2, and so on.

FIGURE 6.4

The coach decides what type of pass the players will make. The drill is run for

97

a certain numbers of passes per player or for a set time.

Details to Teach and Underline
- Make sure the hands are ready to catch and pass immediately.
- Do not make any extra moves before passing.
- Make crisp and accurate passes.

Variation
The drill can be started with two balls at the same time. Any time the coach whistles, the players change the direction of the pass, from right to left, and vice versa.

FOUR-CORNERS DRILL

Aim

98 The aim of the four-corners drill is to practice passing and work on the proper footwork.

Equipment
- 1 ball
- 1 chair

Personnel
- The entire team

How to Run the Drill
Divide the team into four groups of four players per group. The four groups form a rectangle, with a chair in the middle of the rectangle. Player 1 passes a two-hand chest pass (or another pass decided by the coach) to 2, in this case, then

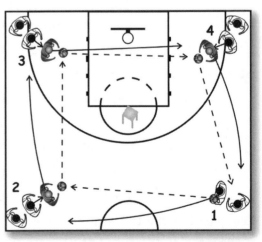

FIGURE 6.5

follows the pass and goes to the end of 2's line.

As soon as 2 has received the ball, the player pivots on the inside foot, fronts the chair, makes a jab step and then a shot fake, turns toward 3, and passes the ball to the teammate, and so on, as shown in Figure 6.5. The drill is run for a certain numbers of passes or for a set time.

Details to Teach and Underline
- Be ready to receive the ball.
- Make an effective and game-condition sweep of the ball and shot fake, with the ball at forehead level, at the same time bending the knees.
- Always maintain balance on all the movements.

Variation
The drill can also be performed adding more balls, for a maximum of four. To simulate a game situation, one defender, who defends at 50 percent, can be added in front of each group.

HIT-THE-TARGET DRILL

Aim
Basketball is a game of precision, and the aim of the hit-the-target drill is to be very accurate while passing, hitting a precise target.

Equipment
- 1 ball per player

Personnel
- The entire team
- Two coaches

How to Run the Drill
The team is aligned in front of a wall, with one ball per player. Use two pieces of

tape to make a cross in front of each player, which functions as a target. Two coaches are set behind the line to make the necesary corrections.

The players are set from 12 to 15 feet away from the wall, and they must hit the target with a certain type of pass chosen by the coach, as shown in Figure 6.6. The drill is run for 3 or 6 minutes, the type of pass changed every 1 or 2 minutes.

Details to Teach and Underline

- Keep the same mechanics and accuracy from the first to the last pass.
- Make the pass using the whole body, not just the hands and the arms.

Variation

100 The players can count the number of times they hit the target in the amount of time decided by the coach.

The coach divides the team in two groups, and the group that hits the target more times in a set time wins and the losers do sprints. One coach per group records the number of targets hit.

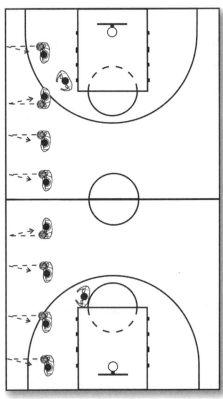

FIGURE 6.6

PASSING-ON-MOVING DRILL

Aim

The aim of the passing-on-moving drill is to practice footwork and passing to a teammate, who is moving randomly.

Equipment

- 1 ball for every two players

Personnel

- The entire team

How to Run the Drill

Divide the team into pairs of two players, 10 to 15 feet apart from each other, with one ball per pair. The pairs are spread out on the half-court.

FIGURE 6.7

One player with the ball stands in front of his teammate, who is moving randomly from the right to the left, and vice versa. The passer, pivoting on the pivot foot, makes two ball fakes with jab steps, and then passes the ball, with the type of pass decided by the coach, to a teammate, who is constantly moving laterally, as shown in Figure 6.7. The drill is run from 2 to 4 minutes.

101

Details to Teach and Underline

- Use effective and real ball fakes before passing, as in a game, from the beginning to the end of the drill.
- The receiver must always offer a target to the passer, either one or two hands.

Variation

The players change the type of pass, called by the coach, after one minute.

PASS-AND-FOLLOW-IN-TRAFFIC DRILL

Aim

The aim of the pass-and-follow-in-traffic drill is to prepare the players to pass, catch, and sprint in traffic.

Equipment

- 2 balls

Personnel

- Eight players

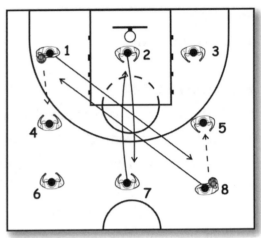

FIGURE 6.8

How to Run the Drill

Set the players in a rectangle on one half-court, as shown in Figure 6.8, with one ball in the hands of each of two players standing opposite each other, in this case, 1 and 8. These two players pass the ball at the same time, using the pass decided by the coach, to the teammate on their right, respectively to 4 and 5, and then they sprint to exchange the positions: 1 goes to 8's spot, 8 to 1's spot, and so on.

The drill lasts from 3 to 5 minutes or for a certain number of passes.

Details to Teach and Underline

- First, make a correct and precise pass, then sprint.
- Do not stand still after the pass, but instead sprint to the new position, immediately after the ball has left the hands of the passer.
- The receiver must go toward the ball with his hands before the ball has left the hands of the passer.

Variation

Adding another ball creates a more difficult drill. The drill can be run using the entire court.

LEFT- AND RIGHT-HAND DRILL

Aim

The aim of the left- and right-hand drill is to practice a one-hand push-pass.

Equipment

- 2 balls for every 2 players

Personnel

- The entire team

How to Run the Drill

Divide the team into pairs of two players, facing each other 10 to 15 feet apart, with one ball for every two players. Three pairs of players are in one half-court, and three are in the other half-court.

The players pass each other the ball with one hand, alternatively with the left and then with the right hand. After each pass, they slide until they reach the mid-court line, and then they repeat the drill until they reach the spot where they started the drill, as shown in Figure 6.9. They repeat the drill two or three times.

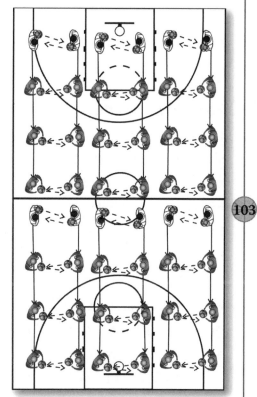

Details to Teach and Underline

- Completely extend the hand while passing.

FIGURE 6.9

- Keep knees bent for the entire drill.
- Be ready in advance to receive the ball with one hand.

Variation

At the beginning, the players slide slowly, then, when they have mastered the one-hand pass, they increase the speed of the lateral slides.

TWO-WHEEL DRILL

Aim

The aim of the two-wheel drill is to practice passing and to improve peripheral vision.

Equipment

■ 2 balls

Personnel

■ The entire team

How to Run the Drill

Divide the team into two groups of five or six players each. One group forms a circle around the jump-ball area, and the other forms a larger circle around the first one. Each group has a ball. The inner group rotates clockwise, and the second one rotates in the opposite direction. While rotating, each group passes the ball to the other group, using the pass decided by the coach, as shown in Figure 6.10.

The drill is run from 2 to 4 minutes. At the whistle, the two groups change the direction of the rotation.

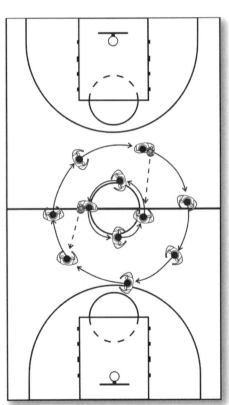

FIGURE 6.10

Details to Teach and Underline

■ Use always peripheral vision to pass and receive the ball.

■ Always attempt a perfect pass, even in a difficult situation such as this one.

■ Move toward the ball when the player is about to receive it.

104

Variation

The players increase the speed of the rotation. After 1 minute, the coach changes the type of pass.

PASSING AND CUTTING DRILL

Aim

The aim of the passing and cutting drill is to get used to different types of passing and cutting.

Equipment

- 2 balls

Personnel

- The entire team

FIGURE 6.11.a

How to Run the Drill

Divide the team into three lines: one near the left sideline at the free-throw line extension, with player 5 with a ball; one at the left corner of the half-court, and one near the right corner, with player 1 with a ball. Player 3 is on the right corner of the free-throw area, and player 4 is outside the three-point line, in front of 3.

Player 1 passes the ball to 4 and cuts toward the three-second lane, in between 4 and 3. Player 4 passes to 3, and cuts around him. Player 3 passes to 1, who drives to the basket, finishing with a layup, as shown in Figure 6.11a. After

FIGURE 6.11.b

the layup, 1 moves to the position of 3, while 4 gets the rebound.

At the same time 1 passes to 4, 5 passes to 7, and 7 passes to 2. Then, the drill is run with the same pattern, as shown in Figure 6.11b. The drill is run for a certain numbers of layups or for a set time.

Details to Teach and Underline

- Pass the ball quickly.
- Make crisp and angled cuts.

Variation

The players must score a certain numbers of layups in a given amount of time.

FOUR-CORNERS DRILL

Aim

The aim of the four-corners drill is to practice passing full court and shooting.

Equipment

- 3 balls

Personnel

- The entire team
- Two coaches

How to Run the Drill

Set four lines of players in the four corners of the court, with two coaches in the jump-ball area, facing the baskets. Player 2, in the middle lane, passes the ball to 3 and follows the pass, while 1 sprints in the middle of the court, receives the ball from 3, and passes to the coach. Then, the three players make defensive slides back to the basket, as shown in Figure 6.12a.

Then, as the coach passes the ball to 1, they run the fast break: 1 passes to 2 and runs in the right lane, 2 makes a long pass to 3, who has sprinted and fin-

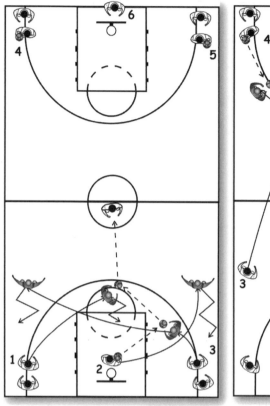

FIGURE 6.12.a

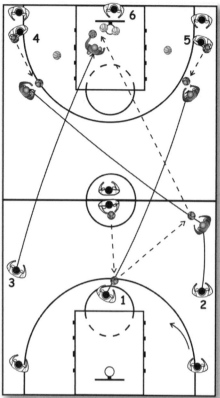

FIGURE 6.12.b

ished with a layup, and 2, after the pass, runs in the left lane. Players 1 and 2 receive, respectively, from 5 and 4 and finish with jump shots, as shown in Figure 6.12 b. Then, 4, 5, and 06 step in and run the drill at the opposite basket.

Details to Teach and Underline

- Carefully make the passes and perform the proper defensive slides.
- Watch always the ball while it's in the air and until it is in the hands, and be ready to catch the ball with both hands.
- Don't make sloppy layups or jump shots.

WAVE-AND-THREE-SHOT DRILL

Aim

The aim of the wave-and-three-shot drill is to have the players work on passing while running and then shooting.

Equipment

- 4 balls

Personnel

- The entire team

How to Run the Drill

Set three lines of three players along one baseline, and one line on the opposite baseline, as shown in Figure 6.13. Player 1 has the ball, while on the opposing line players 4, 5, and 6 have one ball each.

Players 1, 2, and 3 make a wave from one baseline toward the other one, with one player finishing with a layup, while the other two receive the balls from 4 and 6 and make jump shots. Then, 4, 5, and 6 run the same pattern. The drill ends after a certain numbers of shots, or after a set time.

Details to Teach and Underline

- Run at full speed.
- No dribbling is allowed.
- Make crisp passes and hit the target shown by the receiver.

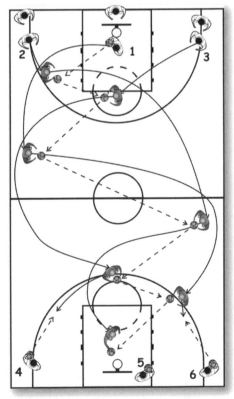

FIGURE 6.13

108

Variation

The players change the type of shots; for example, the two players on the wings drive to the basket, while the player in the middle makes a jump shot.

FOUR PLAYERS PASSING-AND-MOVING DRILL

Aim

The aim of the four players passing-and-moving drill is to practice passing, while coordinating the moves.

Equipment

- 3 balls

Personnel

- The entire team

How to Run the Drill

Divide the team into four groups of three players each, set on one half-court. Two groups are in the corners and two are on the left- and right-wing spots, as shown in Figure 6.14. The players on the right corner have one ball each.

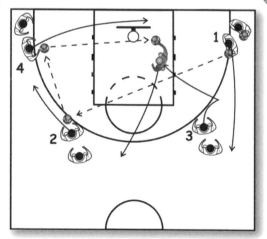

FIGURE 6.14

Player 1 makes a skip pass to 2, who makes a quick pass to 4. As soon as the ball leaves the hands of 1, 3 fakes a cut to the corner, then cuts to the basket, receives from 4, and finishes with a layup. Player 4 gets the rebound.

This is the rotation: 1 goes to 3's line, 3 goes to 2's line, 2 goes to 4's line, and 4 to 1's line. The drill is run for a certain number of shots or for a set time. The drill is also run on the left side of the half-court.

Details to Teach and Underline

- Run at full speed.
- No dribbling is allowed.
- Make crisp passes and hit the target shown by the receiver.

Variation

The drill is run with two balls. Player 2, opposite 1, has another ball and passes it to 4, who makes a jump shot. Then, the drill is run in the same way. The players can also make different types of shots, with or without a dribble before.

PASSING-CONTEST DRILL

Aim

The aim of the passing-contest drill is to run a drill that is a contest, working at passing under game conditions with the defense.

110

Equipment

- 1 ball

Personnel

- The entire team

How to Run the Drill

Divide the team into two squads of five players each, one on defense and the other on offense, as shown in Figure 6.15. The offensive players pass the ball to each other, and, after each pass, they change their positions. No lob or skip passes are permitted. The defenders must try to deflect, touch, or steal the ball.

One point is assigned to the offense

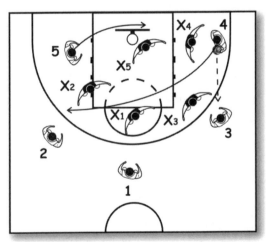

FIGURE 6.15

for every successful pass, and one point is assigned to the defense if the pass is deflected, touched, or stolen. The team that first reaches a certain number of points wins. The losers do sprints.

Details to Teach and Underline
- Use fakes before passing.
- Make sharp and angled cuts.

Variation
The drill is run for a set amount of time, and the winner is the team with the most points at the end of the time.

AROUND-THE-CHAIRS DRILL
Aim
The aim of the around-the-chairs drill is to practice passing full court and shooting when tired.

Equipment
- 3 balls

Personnel
- The entire team

How to Run the Drill
Divide the team into three groups set at the baseline, two in the corners, and the third one in the middle lane, with three balls. Two chairs are set on the opposite half-court near the three-point line.

Player 2 fakes a cut to the three-second

FIGURE 6.16

lane, then sprints to the other basket and receives the ball from 1 outside the three-point line. After the pass to 2, 1 sprints in the middle lane of the court; 3 fakes a cut in the three-second lane, then sprints in the left lane, receives a long pass from 2, and finishes with a layup.

After the pass to 3, 2 circles around the two chairs, sprints back to the basket where he started the drill, receives the ball back from 1, who got the rebound of the 3's shot, and drives to the basket, finishing with a layup, as shown in Figure 6.16.

Details to Teach and Underline

- Sprint from the beginning to the end of the drill.
- Make always crisp passes.

Variation

The players make jump shots instead of layups.

BALL-REVERSAL DRILL

Aim

The aim of the ball-reversal drill is to help the players improve the quick ball-reversal passes.

Equipment

- 4 balls

Personnel

- The entire team

How to Run the Drill

Divide the team into four groups, one of inside players, and three of perimeter players. The group of inside players is set outside the baseline, with one inside player on the low post. The groups of perimeter players are set in this way: one group on the left-wing spot with the balls, one group on the right-wing spot, and one group in the middle of the court. One coach or a player is under the basket and rebounds the ball. Two defenders defend at 50 percent on players 1 and 5.

FIGURE 6.17a

Player 1 passes a first ball to 5, who makes a hard dribble toward the middle of the court and passes to 2. Player 3 first fakes a cut to the corner, goes back, receives the ball from 2, and makes a three-point shot, as shown in Figure 6.17a.

The same four players run the second part of the drill, as shown in Figure 6.17b: 1, who has another ball on the floor, passes to 5, 2 fakes a cut away from the ball and then goes back, receives from 5 and makes a three-point shot, while 3 relocates.

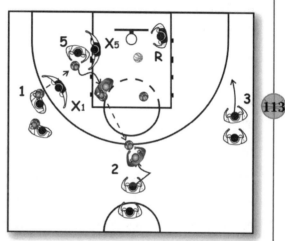

FIGURE 6.17b

This is the rotation: 5 goes at the end of the baseline group, 1 at the end of 2's group, 2 at the end of 3's group, and 3 at the end of 1's group.

The drill is run also on the right side of the half-court. The drill is run for a certain numbers of shots or for a set time.

Details to Teach and Underline

- Make crisp and accurate passes.
- Move and shoot at game speed.

113

Variations

- The players make a dribble or a shot fake and a dribble before shooting.
- They make a middle-range jump shot instead of a three-point shot.

FIVE PLAYERS PASSING DRILL

Aim

The aim of the five players passing drill is to practice passing and to coordinate the movements in a game situation.

Equipment

- 2 balls

Personnel

- The entire team

FIGURE 6.18

How to Run the Drill

The team is divided into two groups of five players each, each group set in one half-court, with one ball per group.

Player 1 passes to 2, who passes to 4, and then receives a screen from 3. Player 2 goes around the screen, cuts in the lane, receives from 4, and finishes with a layup. Player 2 gets his own rebound, and makes an outlet pass to 5, as shown in Figure 6.18.

This is the rotation: 1 goes to 2's spot, 2 to 5's spot, 3 to 4's spot, and 5 to 1's spot. The drill ends when all the players have finished with a layup. The drill is repeated on the left side.

Details to Teach and Underline

- Make crisp and accurate passes.
- Move and shoot at game speed.

Variation

The player, who receives the screen, instead of cutting in the lane, fades away from the screen, receives the pass, and shoots from outside.

THREE PLAYERS–TWO BALLS DRILL

Aim

The aim of the three players–two balls drill is to work on passing, cutting, and shooting.

Equipment

- 4 balls
- 1 chair

Personnel

- The entire team

How to Run the Drill

Divide the team into three groups, one in the middle lane of the court with two balls, one in the right corner with two balls, and one on the left-wing spot. One chair is set near the three-point line laterally to the group in the middle lane of the court.

Player 1 starts to dribble toward the chair, then, with a crossover dribble (or another type of dribble, such as the behind-the-back or between-the-legs dribble), changes the pace and direction, passes the ball to 3, and sprints to the right corner of the free-throw area. Player 1 receives the ball from 2, and then passes the ball back to 2, who, after the pass to 1, fakes a high cut to make a backdoor cut to the basket. Player 2 finishes with a layup.

Right after the pass to 2, 1 sprints to the left corner of the free-throw area, receives from 3, and makes a jump shot, as shown in Figure 6.19. The drill is repeated on the left side of the half-court and ends after a certain number of shots or after a set time.

This is the rotation: 2, after getting the rebound of his own shot, passes the ball to 1's line and goes at the end of 3's line, 3 gets the rebound of 1's shot and go to 2's line, and 1 goes to the end of 3's line.

FIGURE 6.19

Details to Teach and Underline

- Make crisp and accurate passes.
- Move and shoot at game speed.

Variation

Both players 2 and 1 shoot jump shots or both finish with the layup, so they can also work on communication when shooting in traffic.

116

HAND-OFF-PASS DRILL

Aim

The aim of the hand-off-pass drill is to get used to make hand-off and full-court passes.

Equipment

- 8 balls

Personnel

- The entire team

How to Run the Drill

Divide the team into four groups: two groups are set on the left and right sides of the three-second lane, facing the mid-court line, with four balls per line. One group is near the mid-court line, and one at the three-point line on the opposite basket, on the left side of the court.

Player 2 passes to 3, then sprints to the opposing basket. Player 1 passes to 2, then sprints to the opposing basket toward 3. Player 1 receives a hand-off pass from 3, makes a couple of dribbles, and passes to 2, who drives to the basket and finishes with a layup.

Right after the pass to 2, 1 receives a hand-off pass from 3, makes a couple of dribbles, passes to 4, receives a hand-off pass, and shoots a jump shot, as shown in Figure 6.20.

This is the rotation: 3 and 4 get the rebounds of the shots of 1 and 2, then they go, respectively, to the end of 1's and 2's lines, while 1 and 2 go, respectively, to the end of 4's and 3's lines.

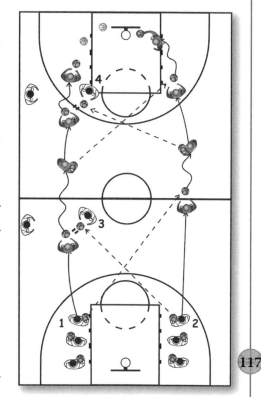

FIGURE 6.20

The drill is also run on the right side of the court and ends after a certain numbers of shots or after a set time.

Details to Teach and Underline

- Sprint to the opposite basket.
- Grab the ball hard with both hands on the hand-off passes.
- Make crisp and sharp long passes.
- When dribbling after the hand-off passes, avoid traveling, and make a long and hard dribble.

Variations

The players on both lines makes jump shots or layups. The two lines compete on which line scores more baskets in a set time.

117

FOUR-LANE PASSING DRILL

Aim

The aim of the four-lane passing drill is to practice passing while running at full speed.

Equipment

- 8 balls

Personnel

- The entire team

How to Run the Drill

Divide the team into four groups, set near the baseline: one group in the left corner, one near the left short corner of the three-second lane, one on the right short corner of the three-second lane, and one in the right corner. The balls are in the hands of the two inside groups' players, 2 and 3.

Players 2 and 3 start the drill by passing, respectively, to 1 and 4. Right after the passes, 2 and 3 cross each other and receive passes from 4 and 1, who run along the baseline. The drill ends at the other basket, where 2 and 3 make jump shots, as shown in Figure 6.21.

After the shot, 2 and 3 go on the corners and 1 and 4 go near the short corners of the three-second lane, starting the drill again after all the groups have run the drill.

The drill is run for a given numbers of back-and-forth executions.

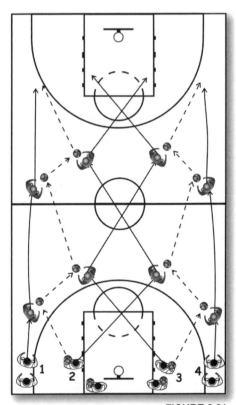

FIGURE 6.21

118

Details to Teach and Underline

- Run at full speed.

- Pass and receive with two hands.

- Pass the ball forward to a teammate.

Variation

The two inside players both shoot layups.

7
Perimeter Players' Drills

Basketball is the ultimate "team sport," perhaps more than any other team sport, such as soccer, volleyball, or baseball. It is a sport where all five players on the court work together and all five teammates are involved. But, during the course of the game, every player on offense has the chance to get the ball and play one-on-one with his defender. The player needs the proper moves in his arsenal to get open and receive the ball, then to beat the defender and drive to the basket or create space for a noncontested jump shot. Otherwise, he can be a detriment to his team, because his defender will not cover him and will jam the lane, or double-team a more dangerous player.

In this chapter, we will describe the drills for the perimeter players. We will discuss exercises that show how to get free and how to create space in order to work one-on-one, two-on-two, and three-on-three, and how to improve footwork and shooting.

In today's game, where the perimeter player can also play inside, and the inside players come out of the lane, we think that the inside players should also run these specific drills that are run for the perimeter players. They will benefit by improving their knowledge of the game, as well as their skills, adding another dimension to their game.

JAB-STEP DRILLS

Mastering the jab-step, in combination with all the other moves, is basic for every effective offensive player. The aggressive jab-step creates a reaction by the defender, so the player on offense must be able to read the situation immediately and attack with the proper countermove. Do not underestimate this basic move because, if a player has mastered the jab-step series, he can become very dangerous and unpredictable on one-on-one on offense.

JAB-STEP STATIONARY DRILL

Aim

The aim of the jab-step stationary drill is to practice the basic jab-step and the fake, important tools for any offensive player.

Equipment

- 1 ball per player

Personnel

- The entire team
- Two coaches

How to Run the Drill

Spread out the team in the half-court, with one ball per player, and the coach in front of the players. The players have the ball on their right side in the triple-threat position, as shown in Figure 7.1. At the coach's signal, each player performs a strong and aggressive jab-step.

This is the series:

- The players perform five jab-steps, going forward with the right foot, the ball in the right hand, and then five jab-steps, going forward with the left foot, the ball in the left hand, with no dribble.
- Same routine, but now they take a strong first-step drive (see Chapter 2, Basic Footwork and Cuts) with the same hand and foot, first right and then left.

121

- Same routine, but now they sweep the ball from one side to the other and make a strong first-step drive, dribbling with the other hand, first right and then left.
- Same routine, but now, after sweeping the ball and making a direct drive, they make a crossover dribble, first right and then left.
- Same routine, but now, after the jab-step and the shot fake, they make a strong first-step drive, same hand and foot, first right and then left.
- Same routine, but now, after the jab-step, they make a shot fake, then a strong lateral dribble, and go up as if making a jump shot, first right and then left.
- Same routine, but now they make a side jab-step, not forward, and then a strong first-step drive, first right, then left.

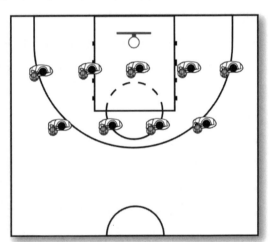

FIGURE 7.1

Details to Teach and Underline

122

- Imagine making the jab-step at the defender's ankle.
- Do not overextend the jab-step leg.
- Look at the defender, not the floor.
- At the beginning of the move, hold the ball on the side of the body, between the hip and the chest.
- Also fake with the ball, without exposing it too much.
- Protect the ball with the inside shoulder.
- When sweeping the ball, make a very quick move, bringing the ball low from one side to the other side of the body, below the knees, and changing the upper hand on the ball at the same time.
- Fake a real shot, bringing the ball to forehead level, and, at the same time, bending the legs.
- Make a strong first-step, matched with the first dribble.

SELF-PASS, TURN, AND JAB-STEP DRILL

Aim

The aim of the self-pass, turn, and jab-step drill is to help the players master the jab-step series at the coach's command.

Equipment

- 1 ball per player

Personnel

- The entire team
- A coach

How to Run the Drill

Form two or three lines of players, about 15 feet apart. Each player has a ball, and the coach is in front of them, as shown in Figure 7.2. The players make a self-pass, sprint to catch the ball, make a one-count stop, turn toward the basket, and perform one of the jab-step moves requested by the coach.

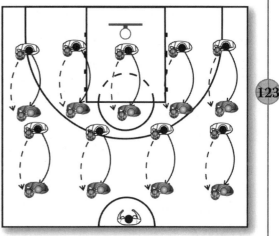

FIGURE 7.2

JAB-STEP-WITH-THE-DEFENDER DRILL

Aim

The aim of the jab-step-with-the-defender drill is to move the jab-step series up to the next level, with a defender in front.

Equipment

- 4 balls

123

Personnel

- The entire team

How to Run the Drill

Divide the team into four groups: one group near the low left corner of the three-second lane, another one on the low right corner, one in the guard spot on the left with the balls, and another on the guard spot on the right with the balls.

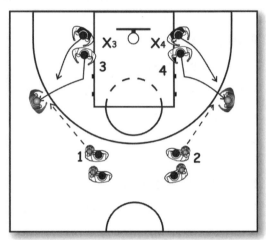

FIGURE 7.3

Player 3 makes an L cut, followed by X3, who defends at 50 percent. Player 1 passes the ball to 3, who reads the position of the defender X3 and makes the proper jab-step move, then drives to the basket or makes a jump shot.

124

Then, 4 and X4 run the same pattern, as shown in Figure 7.3. After 3's and 4's shots, X3 and X4 become offensive players, while 3 goes to the end of the 1's line, and 4 to the end of 2's line. Players 1 and 2 go, respectively, to the end of 3's and 4's lines.

The drill ends after a certain number of shots or a set time.

Details to Teach and Underline

- Immediately notice how the defender covers the offensive player and which foot he has forward.
- Make a jab-step to the defender's ankle.
- Don't overextend the jab-step.
- Make a jab-step in a crouched position if the defender is very tight.
- Jab and go if there is no reaction by the defender to the jab-step.

- Turn the shoulder and get "slimmer" when driving past the defender.
- Make the first dribble with the ball bouncing over the hip of the defender.

Variation

The offensive players make a V step to get open. The defenders play at game speed and as if under game-like conditions.

ROLL-THE-BALL DRILL

Aim

The aim of the roll-the-ball drill is to to practice one-on-one in a game-like situation.

Equipment

- 1 ball

Personnel

- The entire team
- A coach

How to Run the Drill

The team is divided into two groups, set at the two wing spots, on the left and right of the half-court, while the coach with the ball is under the basket.

The coach rolls the ball toward the free-throw line. As the coach shouts, "Go," the first player on the left line and the first player on the right line sprint to catch the ball. The player who gets the ball is on offense, and the other one is on defense, as shown in Figure 7.4.

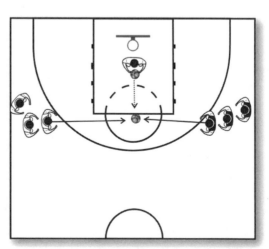

FIGURE 7.4

125

They play one-on-one only in the middle of the court. No more than three dribbles are allowed before shooting. The two players involved must score a basket, either by the player on offense or by the defender, if he has stolen the ball or grabbed the rebound. If the ball goes out of bounds, the two players go to the end of their respective lines. The drill ends after a certain number of one-on-ones, baskets scored, or a set amount of time.

Details to Teach and Underline
- Sprint to catch the ball.
- Don't hesitate or be afraid to dive to the floor and fight for possession of the ball.

Variation
The drill can be run on different spots of the floor, such as with one line in the corner and the other one on the wing, or two lines in the opposite corners of the half-court.

POP-OUT AND V-CUT DRILL

Aim
The aim of the pop-out and-V-cut drill is to practice two different situations to get open and shoot.

Equipment
- 6 balls
- 3 chairs

Personnel
- The entire team

How to Run the Drill
Divide the team into three groups, two outside the baseline and one in the

middle of the half-court. The latter group has two balls for every player. One chair is set at the low-post position on the left side of the three-second lane, one chair is 3 to 4 feet away from the three-second lane on the right side of the half-court, and one chair is at the three-point line, in the middle of the half-court.

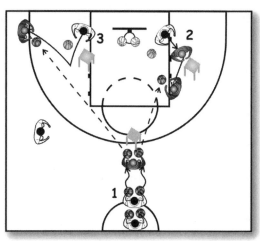

FIGURE 7.5

Player 1 starts to pump-dribble alternately with the two balls. In the meantime, 3 fakes a cut inside the lane, and then, as he gets out of a screen, pops out in the short corner, while 2 makes a V cut and sprints to the corner of the right free-throw area. When 1 reaches the chair, he makes a one-hand pass to 2 and then a one-hand pass to 3. Both players catch and make a jump shot, as shown in Figure 7.5. The drill ends after a certain numbers of shots, or after a set amount of time.

This is the rotation: 1 goes to the end of 2's line, 2 to the end of 3's line, and 3 to the end of 1's line.

Details to Teach and Underline
- Pump the dribble hard.
- Make crisp, one-hand passes to the shooters.
- Change the pace and make angled cuts before receiving the ball.
- Have the feet and body ready to catch and shoot, and don't adjust the position after receiving the ball.

Variation
The players receive and both drive to the basket.

DRIVE, STEP BACK, AND SHOOT DRILL

Aim

The aim of the drive, step back, and shoot drill is to practice receiving the ball while running, then how to drive, step back and shoot.

Equipment

- 6 balls
- 3 chairs

Personnel

- The entire team

How to Run the Drill

Divide the team into three groups. The first group is in the middle of the half-court, with two balls per player. The second group is on the left, and the third group is on the right on the wing spot. One chair is set in front of each of the three groups.

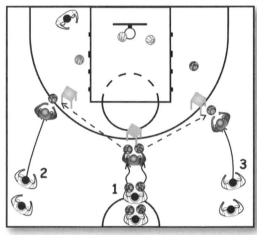

FIGURE 7.6

Player 1 pound-dribbles the balls alternately, and, when he reaches the chair, he makes a one-hand push pass to 2 and a one-hand push pass to 3, who has made a hard cut to the basket at the free-throw line extended. Both players catch, make a hard drive, then a step-back and a jump shot, as shown in Figure 7.6.

The drill ends after a certain numbers of shots, or a set amount of time. This is the rotation: 1 goes to the end of 2's line, 2 to the end of 3's line, and 3 to the end of 1's line.

Details to Teach and Underline

- Pump the dribble hard.
- Make crisp, one-hand passes to the shooters.

128

- Change the pace and make angled cuts before receiving the ball.
- Have the feet and the body ready to catch and shoot, and don't adjust the position after receiving the ball.

Variation

The players receive and make a different type of dribble before shooting.

SELF-PASS, CATCH, AND SQUARE DRILL

Aim

The aim of the self-pass, catch, and square drill is to work on quick catches and square moves, followed by a jump shot or a drive.

Equipment

- 1 ball per player

Personnel

- The entire team
- A coach

How to Run the Drill

Divide the team into two groups, set at the lower corners of the free-throw lane, each player with one ball, while the coach is outside the three-point line. The first player on each line makes a self-pass, bouncing the ball at the corner of the free-throw area, sprints to catch the ball, and then reverses and squares himself to the basket, as shown in Figure 7.7.

The coach calls out certain moves or

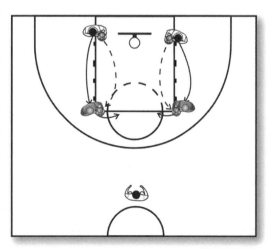

FIGURE 7.7

shots to the players. After finishing with a drive or a jump shot, the two players get their own rebounds and go at the end of the line opposite the line where they started the drill.

Details to Teach and Underline

- Square to the basket with an aggressive and strong move, using the reverse or the front pivot, as requested by the coach.
- Keep knees bent from the time the ball is caught until the end of the move.
- Get the ball in the triple-threat position, and protect it as if guarded by a defender.

Variation

The two lines of players can be set on different spots on the half-court, for example, one in the corner and the other one in the wing spot, and so on.

130

OUTLET PASS, CATCH, SQUARE, AND FAKE DRILL

Aim

The aim of the outlet pass, catch, square, and fake drill is to master different offensive moves with and without the ball.

Equipment

- 4 balls

Personnel

- The entire team
- Two coaches

How to Run the Drill

Divide the team into three groups of two players each in one half-court, and three groups of two players each on the other half-court. One group is under the basket with one ball, another one is in the middle of the half-court, and one is on the right wing spot, while a coach with a ball is on the left-wing spot.

Player 1 tosses the ball to the backboard, grabs the rebound, and passes the ball to 2, who has previously made a V cut. As soon as 2 catches the ball, he squares to the basket, makes an aggressive jab-step and shot fake, and then passes to 3, who has previously made a V cut. Player 3 passes to the player on the line under the basket, as shown in Figure 7.8.

The drill is run for a certain amount of repetitions or after a set amount of time. The drill is also repeated on the left side of the half-court.

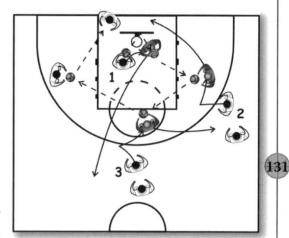

FIGURE 7.8

Details to Teach and Underline
- Change the pace on the cut and on the drive to the basket.
- Finish with the layup with no more than one dribble.

Variation
The players make another type of dribble when driving to the basket, such as a behind-the-back or a between-the-legs dribble. The defender defends aggressively, and decides how to cover the offensive player.

PASSING- AND SHOOTING-ON-HELP DRILL
Aim
The aim of the passing- and shooting-on-help drill is to work on reading help situations and reacting accordingly.

Equipment
- 4 balls
- 4 chairs

131

FIGURE 7.9a

FIGURE 7.9b

Personnel

- The entire team
- Two coaches

FIGURE 7.9c

How to Run the Drill

Divide the team into two groups, one on each half-court, with two chairs near the left sideline, about 6 feet apart. Each group is set as follows: one line, with two balls, of offensive players, in front of the chairs, one defender in the three-second lane, and one offensive player near the low-post spot, both on the help side. One coach is set outside of the three-point line.

Player 1 dribbles around the chairs and drives toward the baseline. The coach calls the position of the defender. If defender X2 helps to close the penetration, 2 cuts in the middle of the lane, receives from 1, and shoots, as shown in Figure 7.9a.

The drill is then run in the same way, but now 1 drives to the middle of the three-second lane. Defender X2 helps to close the penetration; 2 either cuts in the short corner or behind X2 on the opposite position, receives the ball from 1, and shoots, as shown in Figure 7.9b.

Finally, with the same pattern, now on the drive in the middle of the lane by 1, X1 fakes to help, and 1 must read the situation and react: make a two-count stop and a jump shot, or pass to 2, as shown in Figure 7.9c.

The drill is run for a certain number of repetitions or for a set amount of time. It is also repeated on the right side of the half-court.

Variation

The defender defends as in a game, and decides which defensive move to make.

CATCH AND ONE-ON-ONE DRILL

Aim

The aim of catch and one-on-one drill is to help the players learn to fight for possession of the ball and immediately read the different one-on-one possibilities.

Equipment

- 4 balls
- 4 chairs

Personnel

- The entire team
- Two coaches

How to Run the Drill

Divide the team into four groups. Two groups are set on each half-court, outside the three-point line. Two chairs are set near the corners of the free-throw area, with one ball on the floor in between the free-throw circle and the three-

133

point line, while a coach with a ball is outside the three-point line.

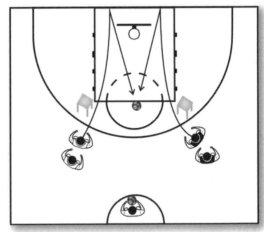

The first two players of the two lines, at the coach's command, sprint, touch the baseline and sprint back. The first player who catches the ball is on offense and the other is on defense. They play one-on-one, using only the central lane of the half-court delineated by the two chairs, as shown in Figure 7.10. Then, the two players go to the end of the line opposite from where they started the drill.

FIGURE 7.10

Two new players begin the drill when the offense has scored a basket or the defense gets the ball on a rebound or a steal. The drill ends after a certain number of one-on-ones per players.

134

Details to Teach and Underline
- Touch the baseline with a foot and a hand.
- Be aggressive when catching the ball and on a rebound on a missed shot.

Variation
The coach can grab the ball and throw it to a spot on the three-second lane, after the two players have touched the baseline. The drill can be also run on different spots of the half-court.

TWO-ON-ONE DRILL
Aim
The aim of the two-on-one drill is to create a more difficult situation than an actual game, using a offensive player to play against two defenders.

Equipment

- 4 balls
- 4 chairs

Personnel

- The entire team
- Two coaches

How to Run the Drill

Divide the team into six groups. Three groups are lined up off the court, along and behind the baseline, on each half-court. One group is on the left corner, one under the basket, and one on the right corner. The players in the left group each have one ball. Two chairs are set a couple of feet away from the corners of the free-throw area. A coach is set outiside of the perimeter.

FIGURE 7.11

As the coach shouts, "Go," the first player on the left group speed-dribbles and turns around the chair, finishing with a shot to the basket; at same time, the player under the basket sprints, touches the mid-court line, and sprints back on defense, while the player on the right corner sprints, turns around the other chair, and recovers on the ball handler. The ball handler tries to score before the arrival of the two defenders, as shown in Figure 7.11. Each player runs the drill for a certain numbers of repetitions, alternating on the three spots, or for a set amount of time.

Details to Teach and Underline

- Make speed-dribbles with as few as possible dribbles, while the defender in the middle line touches the mid-court line with a foot and a hand.

135

ONE-ON-ONE CIRCLING-THE-CHAIRS DRILL

Aim

The aim of the one-on-one circling-the-chairs drill is to work first on demanding conditioning followed by a one-on-one.

Equipment

- 12 chairs
- 6 balls

Personnel

- The entire team
- Two coaches

How to Run the Drill

Divide the team into four groups, one group of defenders and one group of offensive players in the left corner of a half-court, and the same in the right corner on the opposite half-court. In front of each of the two groups, line up three chairs, about 12 feet apart from each other: one chair is set near the free-throw line extension, the second one near the mid-court line, and the third one a couple of feet away from the three-point line on the opposite half-

FIGURE 7.12

court. One coach is on one half-court, and one on the other half-court.

At the coach shouts, "Go," the first defender sprints and circles around the three chairs, while at the same time, the first offensive player speed-dribbles, circling around the chairs on the opposite side, as shown in Figure 7.12.

When the two players reach the third chair, they play one-on-one until the offense scores or the defense gets the ball. Then, the defender goes to the offensive player's line, and vice versa. Each player runs the drill for a certain number of repetitions or for a set amount of time.

Details to Teach and Underline

- Both players must make strong and aggressive first steps (see Chapter 2, Basic Footwork and Cuts).
- The offensive player must speed-dribble, making as few dribbles as possible to go to the basket.

FACE-THE-DEFENDER DRILL

Aim

The aim of the face-the-defender drill is to work on getting free while the defender covers the offensive player face-to-face, in order to play one-on-one.

Equipment

- 4 balls

Personnel

- The entire team
- Two coaches

How to Run the Drill

The team is divided into four groups, two on each half-court, with one group in the middle of the half-court with two balls, and the other one along and outside of the baseline. The group on the baseline is divided alternately with one defender and one offensive player. A coach stands on the perimeter outside of the three-point line.

Player 2 is on offense and player X2 is on defense, facing 1 with the ball. They start the drill in the middle of the three-second lane. Player 1 starts to dribble, and then the coach signals with his hand on which side of the court 2 must get open to play one-on-one, as shown in Figure 7.13.

Player 2 has no more than three seconds to get free, receive the ball from 1, and play one-on-one. If he receives the ball, he can only play in that quarter of the court, and has only three seconds to go to the basket. On the contrary, if the offensive player 2 does not receive the ball in the set time, or if he does not go to the basket in three seconds, he goes to 1's line, X2 goes on offense, and 1 becomes the defender. The drill is run for a certain number of repetitions or for a set amount of time.

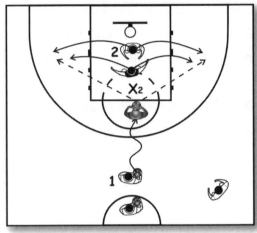

FIGURE 7.13

Details to Teach and Underline

- Don't run continually to get open; instead, change the pace and the direction.
- Don't move in a straight line, but in an angled line.
- Don't watch the passer while trying to get open.
- Show the passer a target—one or two hands—when ready to receive the ball.
- Don't waste time, but immediately read the position of the defender, as soon as the ball is in the hands, and decide which move to do.

Variation

The coach is now positioned under the basket, and the defender guards the offensive player in front. The coach, touching one side of the offensive player's body, gives him a signal on which direction to get out of the lane.

THREE-PASS ONE-ON-ONE DRILL

Aim

The aim of the three-pass one-on-one drill is to teach to the players how to improve their footwork to get open and then play one-on-one on the perimeter.

138

Equipment

- 4 balls

Personnel

- The entire team
- Two coaches

How to Run the Drill

Form two groups of players, one in each half-court, with two balls per group. The players in each group set themselves as follows: two players with the ball in the middle of the half-court, outside of the three-point line; one player on the left and one player on the right side on the wing spot and one defender and one offensive player under the basket, facing the mid court line. A coach is on the perimeter.

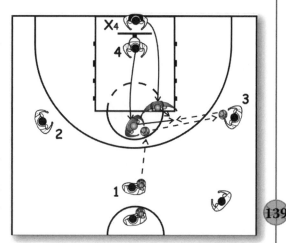

FIGURE 7.14

Player 4 sprints toward 1, who passes the ball to him, while X4 follows 1. The coach shouts, "Right (or left)," 4 makes a reverse to the side called by the coach, passes to 3, cuts toward him, receives the ball back, and plays one-on-one, as shown in Figure 7.14. Then 1 becomes the defender and 3, the offensive player; 2 goes to the end of 1's line, 4 goes on the left of the right-wing spot and X4 goes on the right wing spot.

The player on offense cannot make the same shot twice; for example, if he shoots from a three-point line, once he is on offense again, he can only make a layup or a middle-range jump shot.

The drill is run for a certain number of repetitions per player or for a set amount of time.

Details to Teach and Underline

- Change the pace and the direction to get free.
- Engagè in physical contact with the defender to freeze him and then pop out.
- Square immediately to the basket and protect the ball in the triple-threat postion.

Variation

The drill can be run in different spots on the half-court, such as in the middle of the half-court or in the corner.

"LITTLE TRAIN" SERIES

This is an excellent series of drills to work in sequence on one-on-one, then on two-on-two, and finally on three-on-three.

"LITTLE TRAIN" WITH FOUR PLAYERS DRILL

Aim

The aim of the "little train" with four players drill is to force the ball handler to use the proper footwork and to read the defender's reactions before cutting to the basket, finishing with a layup or playing one-on-one.

Equipment

- 2 balls

Personnel

- The entire team
- Two coaches

How to Run the Drill

Form two groups, each on one half-court. Each group is divided in the following way: two players, 2 and 3 are in the lane under the basket, while 1, facing the mid-court line with the ball, is guarded behind by X1. A coach is set on the perimeter outside the three-point line.

As the coach shouts, "Go," 2 and 3 sprint to the right- and left-wing spots, respectively, and 1 squares to the basket. Then 1 passes the ball to the left or to the right, in this case to the right to 2, and reacts to the reaction of X1:

- He can cut around him.
- He can cut behind him.

As soon as 1 cuts, 3 replaces him in the middle of the half-court, as shown in Figure 7.15a.

If 1 can't receive the ball and go to the basket, he continues the cut, and gets out on the left-wing spot. Player 2 quickly passes the ball to 3, and 3 tries to pass the ball to 1, who has moved to get open, receive, and play one-on-one with X1, as shown in the Figure 7.15b.

When 1 gets his shot, the drill continues until all the three players on offense and the defender have performed the drill.

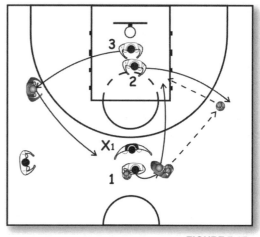

FIGURE 7.15a

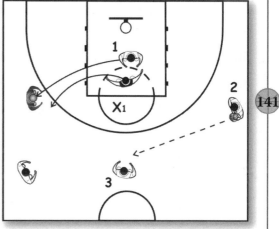

141

FIGURE 7.15b

"LITTLE TRAIN" WITH FIVE PLAYERS DRILL

Aim

The aim of the second step of the "little train" is to practice two-on-two with a passer.

Equipment

- 2 balls

Personnel

- The entire team
- Two coaches

How to Run the Drill

Form two groups, each on one half-court. Each group is divided as follows: three players, 2, 3, and X2, are in the lane under the basket, while one player, 1, facing the mid-court line with the ball, is guarded by X1. A coach is set on the perimeter outside the three-point line. As the coach shouts, "Go," 2, followed by his defender, X2, sprints to the left- (or the right-) wing spot. In this case, 3 will sprint to the left- (or right-) wing spot, and 1 squares to the basket, as shown in Figure 7.16a.

The rules and the pattern are the same, but now they play two-on-two with one passer, as shown in Figure 7.16b.

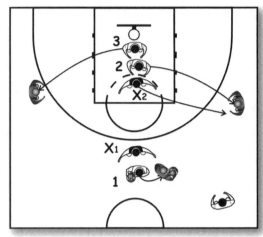

FIGURE 7.16a

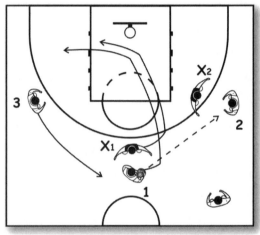

FIGURE 7.16b

"LITTLE TRAIN" WITH SIX PLAYERS DRILL

Aim

The aim of the third and final step of the "little train" drill is to work on a three-on-three under game conditions.

Equipment

- 2 balls

Personnel

- The entire team
- Two coaches

How to Run the Drill

Form two groups, each on one half-court. Each group consists of six players, lined up under the basket, with a coach with the ball on the perimeter outside the three point line. The first, the third, and the fifth players in the line are on offense, while the second, the fourth, and the sixth are on defense. As the coach shouts, "Go," 1, followed by his defender, X1, sprints to the left, to the right-wing spot, or to the middle of the court, while 2 and 3, followed by X2 and X3, will go to the other two open spots on the court, as shown in Figure 7.17a.

The coach passes the ball to one of the offensive players, 2 in this case, and the players play three-on-three, following the same pattern and rules described before, as shown in Figure 7.17 b.

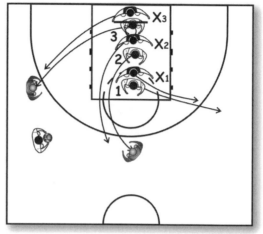

FIGURE 7.17a

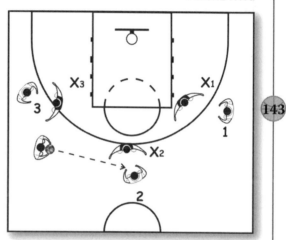

FIGURE 7.17b

143

8

Inside Players' Drills

Today, basketball has begun to depend more on inside players, who get out of the lane, perform pick-and-rolls, and shoot from the outside. Playing inside, with the back to the basket, either in the high or low post, is a forgotten skill.

If an inside player is able to play with his back to the basket, we are convinced that having a player who is able to get open near the basket, as well as to go to rim, based on the reaction of the defense, is still a must in modern basketball. You cannot "teach" a player's size and the height, but you can teach and practice how to play inside.

The drills that we will show in this chapter are designed to help players improve in every aspect of the game, starting with the footwork that is so necessary for every player, but, above all, for the inside players, who must move in narrow and congested spaces. Then, we will cover the different types of shots, the one-on-one, and passing.

FRONT AND REAR TURN, DROP-STEP DRILL

Aim

The front and rear turn, drop-step drill is particularly useful for helping the inside players master basic footwork necessary to play near the basket.

Equipment

- 1 ball for every inside player

Personnel

- All the inside players

How to Run the Drill

The inside players are set near the left sideline, 6 feet away from each other and with one ball each. With the ball at shoulder height, they make a front turn, matched with a sweep of the ball from the shoulder to the waist, pivoting once on the left foot and once on the right foot.

FIGURE 8.1

They repeat the same move in a straight line until they reach the opposite sideline, as shown in Figure 8.1.

Then, following the same pattern, they now make a rear turn. Finally, they make a drop-step.

Details to Teach and Underline

- End each of the moves with the feet parallel.
- Always keep the knees bent from one sideline to the other one on all three moves.
- Look over the opposite shoulder while making the drop-step.

145

- On the drop-step, the drop foot must be behind the front foot.

Variation

The drill is run from baseline to baseline.

CATCH, TURN, AND PASS DRILL

Aim

The aim of the catch, turn, and pass drill is to improve the inside players' footwork and to pass the ball quickly to an open teammate.

Equipment

- 4 balls

Personnel

- The entire team
- Two coaches

How to Run the Drill

Divide the team into four groups of three players each, with one perimeter player on the left- and one on right-wing spot, one inside player at the free-throw line, facing the basket, and one coach with a ball outside the free-throw area. Two groups are on one half-court and the other two on the other one. One ball is set on the floor, behind the inside player, at the top of the free-throw circle,

FIGURE 8.2

As the coach shouts, "Left," the inside player pivots on his left foot, turns, takes a long step, without losing balance, catches the ball, squares back to the basket, and passes the ball to the player on the right-wing spot, as shown in Figure 8.2.

Immediately after the player has caught the ball and passed it, the coach sets another ball on the floor in the same position, and the inside player again runs the drill, now pivoting on the right foot and passing to the player on the left-wing spot. The player makes three left pivot-foot turns and three right-pivot foot turns, then another player steps in.

Detail to Teach and Underline

- While taking a long step to catch the ball, maintain balance.
- Make an aggressive turn, protecting the ball.
- Always keep the knees bent.

Variation

Add a defender on the inside player, who initially guards him 50 percent, and then aggressively.

147

CROSS-STEP-AND-DRIBBLE DRILL

Aim

The aim of the cross-step-and-dribble drill is to create confidence and master the dribble, a fundamental in which inside players are often not too skilled.

Equipment

- 1 ball for every player

Personnel

- All the inside players

How to Run the Drill

Set all the inside players in a line at about the free-throw line extension, with one ball each, held with the right hand at shoulder height. They make a sweep, bringing the ball to waist level, and immediately cross-step with their right foot and pound-dribble with their left hand, as shown in Figure 8.3.

Then they recover the starting position and repeat the same move on the other side. The same pattern is repeated ten times, five times with the right hand and five with the left hand.

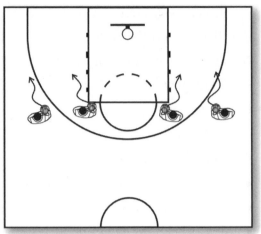

FIGURE 8.3

Details to Teach and Underline

- Do not overextend the cross-step.
- Always maintain balance.
- Make a hard pound-dribble.
- Protect the ball with the other arm bent at a 45-degree angle.

Variation

148 The players make another quick dribble after the first one, then jump stop and repeat the move.

FRONT- AND REAR-TURN, CROSS- AND DROP-STEP DRILL

Aim

The aim of the front- and rear-turn, cross- and drop-step drill is to practice a combined offensive move.

Equipment

- 4 balls

Personnel

- The entire team

How to Run the Drill

The team is divided into four groups, two groups of perimeter players on the left- and right-wing spots, with two balls for each group, while two inside players are set at the low-post spots on the left and right sides, and the other inside players are out of the court along the baseline.

The inside player on the left side asks for the ball, showing his hand as a target. He receives the pass, makes a front turn, a cross-step, and a dribble, followed by a drop-step, and finishes with a dunk, a power shot, or a short-range jump shot, as shown in Figure 8.4.

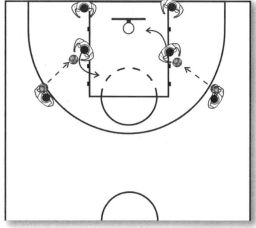

FIGURE 8.4

Then, he repeats the same pattern, but now makes a rear turn. The drill is then run by the other player on the right side. Each player runs the drill five times on the right side and five times on the left.

149

Details to Teach and Underline

- Be aggressive on the movement and in shooting.
- Always keep knees bent for all the moves.

Variation

Add a defender, who covers the inside player at 50 percent at first, and then aggressively.

SKIP-PASS DRILL

Aim

The aim of the skip-pass drill is to improve the footwork and different cuts of the inside players who come from the help side of the court.

Equipment

- 4 balls

Personnel

- The entire team
- Two coaches

How to Run the Drill

Divide the players into six groups of two players each, with one perimeter players' group on the left- and one group on the right-wing spot, one inside players' group in the middle of the half-court, and one coach on the perimeter. The same set is placed in the other half-court.

Player 1 passes the ball to the wing player on the left or the right, as called by the coach, to 2 in this case. Then 1 makes a straight cut to the middle of the three-second lane, until he is under the rim, and makes a diagonal cut, posting up in the low-post position on the ball side.

Player 2 makes a skip pass to 3, and 1 cuts in the middle of the lane and sets himself at the corner of the free-throw area on the ball side, as shown in Figure 8.5a. After a couple of seconds, he pops out and sets a pick on 3. Player 1 decides if he wants to roll on the basket, slip to the basket, or flair out. Player 3 passes the ball to him, and he finishes with a jump shot, a power shot, or a dunk, as shown in Figure 8.5b.

The inside player runs a drill three

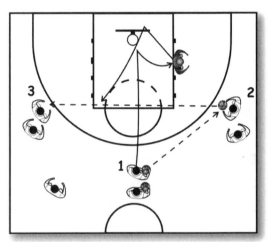

FIGURE 8.5a

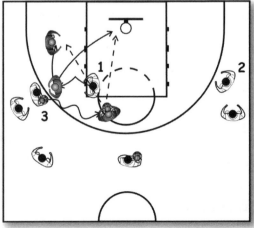

FIGURE 8.5b

150

consecutive times, and then shoots two free-throws. Then he repeats the drill on the other side. Another inside player and two perimeter players step in and start the drill.

Details to Teach and Underline
- Make crisp and angled cuts.
- Change pace; do not go at the same speed.
- Act as if a defender is covering the inside player.
- Always keep knees bent during the drill.
- Go to the basket aggressively.

Variation
Add a defender on the inside player, who initially guards him 50 percent, and then aggressively.

151

OUT-OF-BOUNDS-PASS–TWO-SHOT DRILL
Aim
The aim of the out-of-bounds-pass–two-shot drill is to work on a quick out-of-bounds pass, followed by two different shots, as well as to work on physical conditioning.

Equipment
- 2 balls
- 2 chairs

Personnel
- The entire team

How to Run the Drill
The team is divided into groups of three players, two passers and one inside player, and they work on both half-courts. One chair is set near the mid-court line in the

middle of the half-court, two passers are on the left- and right- wing spots, and one inside player is under the basket, facing it, with the ball.

The inside player makes four hooks under the basket, alternating with the right hand and then with the left hand, without letting the ball hit the floor, and always keeping the ball between his head and chest. Then, he grabs the ball after the last hook shot, runs out-of-bounds, and makes a quick pass to the left, as in this case, or to the right.

Then, he sprints toward the mid-court line, circles around the chair, fakes a cut to the wing spot, cuts aggressively to the three-second lane, receives the ball near the basket, and dunks or makes a power shot, as shown in Figure 8.6a.

Right after the shot, the inside player gets the ball before it hits the floor, goes out-of-bounds, and again makes a pass to the player on the left wing. He repeats the same move, but now receives the ball back at the right corner of the free-throw area, drives hard to the basket, and makes a layup or a dunk, as shown in Figure 8.6b.

The drill is run four times per player, two on the left side, and two on the right, then another inside player and two new passers step in.

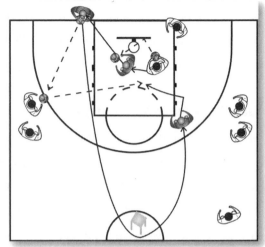

FIGURE 8.6a

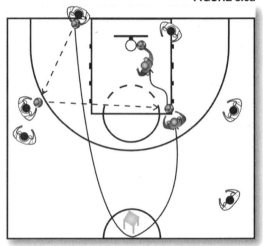

FIGURE 8.6b

Details to Teach and Underline

- Get the rebound aggressively.

- Make the out-of-bound passes as quickly as possible.
- Change pace when going to the basket.

Variation

Ask the inside player to make a different shot, such as jump shot, hook or combined, or with different moves, such as a drop-step, reverse, and so on.

SIX-CHAIR ONE-ON-ONE DRILL

Aim

The aim of the six-chair one-on-one drill is to work on conditioning and on one-on-one with the inside players while they fight for the rebound.

Equipment

- 6 chairs
- 1 ball

Personnel

- All the inside players
- One coach

153

How to Run the Drill

Two lines of three chairs each are set on one half-court, as shown in Figure 8.7, one on the left side and the other one on the right. One chair is on the guard spot, one near the sideline, and one at the corner of the free-throw line. A group of inside players stands in front of each line of chairs, while a coach with a ball stands at the free-throw line.

As the coach shouts, "Go," the first

FIGURE 8.7

two players in each group sprint, circling around the chairs, and when the two players are near the three-second lane, the coach tosses the ball to the backboard. The two players fight for the rebound, and the player who gets the ball is on offense and the other one on defense. The player who gets the ball has 3 seconds to shoot.

The drill ends after a scored basket, either by the offensive player or by the defender, who steals the ball or gets the offensive player's missed shot rebound, or if the offensive player does not score in 3 seconds. After the scored basket, the two players go to the end of the line opposite where they started the drill. The drill is run for a certain number of scored baskets or after a set amount of time.

Details to Teach and Underline

- Always keep the knees bent.
- Do not give up; go to the basket aggressively, even if the defender has an advantage over the offensive player.

Variation

The coach drops the ball to the floor or rolls it, instead of tossing it to the backboard.

EIGHT-SHOT DRILL

Aim

The aim of the eight-shot-drill is to work on continuous shooting from different spots on the court and shooting when fatigued.

Equipment

- 8 balls

Personnel

- All the inside players
- Two rebounders

How to Run the Drill

The inside players are set along the baseline, with one player under the basket, and two rebounders and eight balls are set on the floor around the three-second lane, as shown in Figure 8.8.

The inside player under the basket catches the first ball on the left side and shoots immediately, then catches all the other balls and shoots, without any stops in between. The first player makes the shot decided by the coach: a drop-step and a shot, a jump shot, a layup, a dunk, and so on. Each player makes the same pattern twice, one starting from the right side and one starting from the left side of the half-court.

The rebounders keep score of the missed and made shots, and for every missed shot, the inside player makes one sprint from the baseline to the mid-court line, or from baseline to baseline.

Details to Teach and Underline

- Go to the basket aggressively, from the first to the last shot.
- Do not shoot just to shoot, but to score a basket.
- Use the proper footwork.

Variation

A defender who plays behind the inside player is added: he can first play defense at 50 percent, and then aggressively.

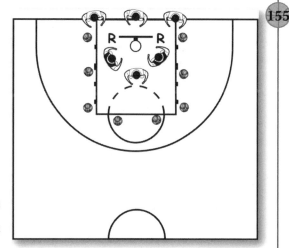

FIGURE 8.8

THREE-CHAIR–THREE-SHOTS DRILL

Aim

The aim of the three-chair–three-shots drill is to improve the shooting ability of the inside players, working on footwork and three different types of shots.

Equipment

- 3 chairs

Personnel

- All the inside players

How to Run the Drill

One chair is set outside the mid-post area on the left side of the three-second lane, the second one in the middle of the free-throw area, and the third one 3 feet away from the three-second lane in the right side of the half-court. One ball is on each of these chairs. A group of inside players is set in front of the third chair, while two rebounders are near the basket.

The first player in the group runs to the chair, picks up the ball, and drives hard to the basket, finishing with a layup or a dunk. Then he sprints to the chair on the left, picks up the ball, makes a reverse, and finishes with a power shot or a jump hook. Finally, he sprints to the chair at the free-throw line, picks up the ball, makes a drop step, and scores a layup or a dunk, as shown in Figure 8.9.

After each player has finished the drill, the two outside chairs are moved to the opposite side, and the drill is run on the right side. Each player runs the drill two times on the right side of the half-court and two times on the left side.

Details to Teach and Underline

- Go to the basket aggressively from the first to the last shot.
- Do not shoot just to shoot, but to score a basket.
- Use the proper footwork.

Variation

The chairs can be moved to different positions around the three-second lane.

FIGURE 8.9

156

A defender in the lane is added: he can first play defense at 50 percent, and then aggressively.

THREE-SPOT-SHOT DRILL

Aim

The aim of the three-spot-shot drill is to improve the speed and the reaction of the inside players, as well as to improve shooting.

Equipment

- 1 ball
- 3 cones

Personnel

- All the inside players
- One coach

How to Run the Drill

The inside players are lined up along the baseline, with one player in the three-sec-ond lane with the ball and the coach on the perimeter, outside the three-second line. There are three spots marked by cones, from where he must shoot: spots 1 and 3 are on the short corners, and 2 is in the lane.

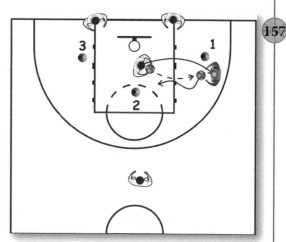

FIGURE 8.10

The coach calls a number, and the player makes a self-pass, catches the ball, squares to the basket, and shoots the shot called by the coach (a jump shot, a hook, a baby hook, a power shot, and so on), as shown in Figure 8.10. Then he scores from the other two spots.

The player ends the drill after he has repeated the pattern for a set number of times decided by the coach.

Details to Teach and Underline

- Go to the basket aggressively from the first to the last shot.
- Do not shoot just to shoot, but to score a basket.
- Use the proper footwork.

Variation

The shots are made from different spots aound the three-second lane. A defender in the lane is added: he can first play defense at 50 percent, and then aggressively.

BASELINE ONE-ON-ONE DRILL

Aim

The aim of the baseline one-on-one drill is to have the inside players practice to play one-on-one in an aggressive way.

Equipment

- 2 balls
- 2 chairs

Personnel

- All the inside players
- One coach

How to Run the Drill

Divide the inside players into two groups, set outside the three-point line, with the first two players of the groups about 5 feet from the corners of the free-throw line. Two chairs are at the mid-post spots, one on the left and the other on the right of the three-second lane, with one ball on each chair.

As the coach shouts, "Go," the two players sprint, touch the baseline, and then go to catch the ball on the left or the right chair, as called by the coach. The player who catches the ball is on offense, the other on defense, as shown in

Figure 8.11. The player who gets the ball has 3 seconds to shoot.

The drill ends after a scored basket, either by the offensive player or by the defender, who steals the ball or gets the rebound of the missed shot by the offensive player, or if the offensive player does not score in 3 seconds. The offensive player who does not shoot in 3 seconds does five push-ups.

After a scored basket, the two players go to the end of the line opposite from where they started the drill. The drill is run for a certain number of scored baskets or after a set amount of time.

FIGURE 8.11

Details to Teach and Underline

- Read the defense.
- Do not rush the shot.
- Do not give up; defend aggressively, even if the offensive player has an advantage over the defender.

Variation

The chairs are set at the high-post spots at the corners of the free-throw area.

X ONE-ON-ONE DRILL

Aim

The aim of the X one-on-one drill is to simulate cuts from the high- and the low-posts, followed by one-on-one.

Equipment

- 1 ball
- 1 chair

Personnel

- All the inside players
- One coach

How to Run the Drill

The inside players are divided into two groups. One player is at the low-post spot and another one at the high-post spot, at the corner of the free-throw area, at the left side of the half-court. The coach is outside the three-point line. One chair with a ball on it, is set 4 feet away from the three-second lane at about the mid-post spot.

FIGURE 8.12

160   As the coach shouts, "Go," the player at the low-post sprints to the high-post spot at right corner of the free-throw area and touches the line with one hand; at the same time, the player at the high post sprints to the low-post spot and touches the last mark of the lane, then both sprint to the chair, as shown in Figure 8.12. The player who gets the ball has 3 seconds to shoot.

The drill ends after a scored basket by the offensive player or by the defender, who steals the ball or gets the offensive player's missed shot rebound, or if the offensive player does not score in 3 seconds. If the offensive player does not shoot in 3 seconds, he does five push-ups.

Then, the two players go to the end of the line opposite from where they started the drill. The drill is run for a certain number of scored baskets or after a set amount of time.

Details to Teach and Underline

- Read the defense.

- Do not rush the shot.
- Do not give up; defend aggressively, even if the offensive player has an advantage over the defender.

Variation

The chairs are set at the high-post spots at the corners of the free-throw area.

CONSECUTIVE PICK-AND-ROLL DRILL

Aim

The aim of the consecutive pick-and-roll drill is to teach the inside players to play pick-and-roll and use proper footwork.

Equipment

- 4 balls

Personnel

- The entire team

How to Run the Drill

The team is divided into three groups, two with perimeter players on the left- and right-wing spots, and one group of inside players out of the court along the baseline, with one inside player under the basket.

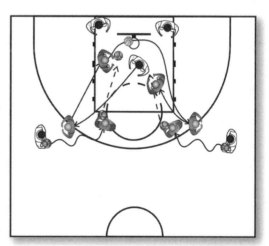

FIGURE 8.13

The inside player under the basket sprints to play pick-and-roll with one of the perimeter players. He sets a screen, rolls to the basket, receives the pass. and finishes with a layup or a dunk. Immediately after, he sprints to play pick-and-roll with the perimeter player on the other wing spot, as shown in Figure 8.13.

The same inside player runs the drill two or three times, for a total of four or six pick-and-rolls.

Details to Teach and Underline

- Pay attention to the angle of the pick.
- On all the pick-and-roll moves, keep the knees bent.
- Preferably, on the roll, the passer should make a bounce pass to the inside player.
- Show the passer the hands as a target.

Variation

A defender on the inside player and a defender on the ball handler are added, and they can first play defense at 50 per cent, and then aggressively.

162 TWO-CHAIR LOW-POST SHOT DRILL

Aim

The aim of the two-chair low-post shot drill is to improve the inside player's speed, while working on his footwork and shooting.

Equipment

- 4 balls
- 4 chairs

Personnel

- The entire team

How to Run the Drill

The team is divided into groups of three players, two rebounders and one inside player under the basket, facing it. They work on both half-courts. One chair is set near the left-side low-post spot, and one on the right-side low-post spot, with one ball on each chair, while two rebounders are on the three-second lane, and a coach in the middle of the court.

The inside player turns to the right, grabs the ball on the chair, and makes one of the following moves, called by the coach, as shown in Figure 8.14, repeating it on the left:

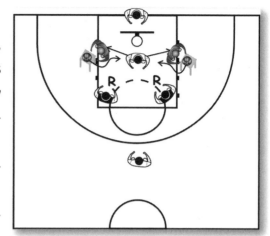

FIGURE 8.14

- A drop-step without a dribble, finishing with a power shot or a dunk
- A reverse and then a hook shot, without a dribble in the middle of the lane
- A drop-step with a dribble toward the baseline, finishing with a power shot or a dunk
- A repeat of the previous move, but toward the middle of the lane
- A reverse and then a jump hook

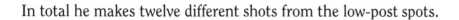

In total he makes twelve different shots from the low-post spots.

Details to Teach and Underline

- Immediately after catching the ball, make a head fake, turning the head to the shoulder opposite the drop-step.
- On a drop-step, turn the drop-step foot, pointing the toes toward the basket.
- After the shot, immediately square to the basket, ready to get the rebound.

Variation

The player makes a fake shot before shooting. A defender in the lane is added: he can first play defense at 50 percent, and then aggressively.

BAD-PASS DRILL

Aim

The aim of the bad-pass drill is to teach the inside players to catch the ball,

163

even if the pass is not perfect, and go to the basket.

Equipment
- 4 balls

Personnel
- All the inside players
- Four passers

How to Run the Drill

Divide the inside players on the two half-courts, with two passers with the balls at each wing spot.

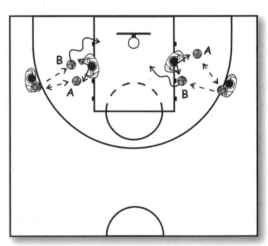

FIGURE 8.15

The passer makes a bad pass to the inside player, who turns to the basket and shoots. He rebounds his own shot, and passes the ball back to the passer, then makes a couple of quick slides, on the left or right side, and repeats the drill, as shown in Figure 8.15.

The drill is run at the same time on both sides of the half-court, so the inside players can also work on shooting in traffic.

Each inside player makes five shots on one side of the half-court and then five shots on the other side.

Details to Teach and Underline
- Always keep the knees bent.
- Immediately after catching the ball, look over the shoulder opposite the direction you want to go.
- Have the hands ready to catch the ball and then set the ball between the chin and the chest.

164

Variation

The drill is run in the same way, but with the inside players set at the high post, near the corners of the free-throw area.

HIGH-POST SHOOTING DRILL

Aim

The aim of the high-post shooting drill is to practice jump shooting from the high-post spots.

Equipment

- 4 balls
- 4 chairs

Personnel

- All the inside players
- Four passers

How to Run the Drill

The inside players are divided into two groups, one group on each half-court, with two rebounders near each three-second lane. Two chairs are set on each half-court, at the corners of the free-throw area, with one ball on each chair.

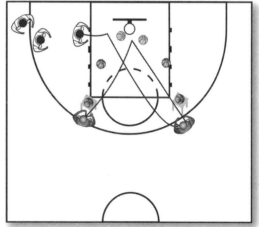

FIGURE 8.16

The first inside player starts the drill at the left low-post spot. He fakes a cut to the basket, then sprints to the chair on the right corner, catches the ball, and makes a jump shot. He follows his shot, fakes a cut, then sprints to the left chair, catches the ball, and makes a second jump shot, as shown in Figure 8.16.

The player makes ten shots, five on the left, and five from the right corner. Then another player steps in.

Details to Teach and Underline

- Change pace and direction before sprinting to the chair.
- Bend the knees before reaching the chair, not after.
- Have the feet pointed toward the basket, after squaring to the basket.
- Don't rush; split the two moves: shoot first, go to the rebound after.

Variation

The player makes a shot fake and one pound-dribble before shooting.

TRAILER SHOOTING DRILL

Aim

The aim of the trailer shooting drill is to improve the inside players' ability to run the court and finish the fast break as a trailer.

Equipment

166

- 4 balls

Personnel

- The entire team

How to Run the Drill

The inside players are divided into two groups, each one on each half-court behind the baseline. Two passers are on the left- and right-wing spots with one ball each.

The first player of the inside players group sets himself on the low post, receives the ball from the passer, passes the ball back, then sprints to the mid-court. He touches the mid-court line

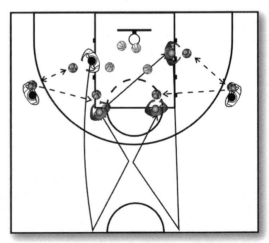

FIGURE 8.17

with his hand, then sprints back, fakes a cut in one direction, changes his direction and pace, stops at the free-throw area, receives the ball, and makes a jump shot, as shown in Figure 8.17.

He then posts down on the other side of the court, receives the ball from the other passer, passes the ball back, and repeats the same pattern. He runs the drill six times, three on the right side and three on the left.

Details to Teach and Underline

- Execute every fundamental perfectly: passing, cutting, and shooting.
- Be prepared to shoot as soon as receiving the ball, not after.
- Always keep the knees bent.

Variation

The player dribbles before shooting.

9

Spacing and Collaboration Drills

I n basketball, because the players are big and fast, the spacing between the offensive players is of paramount importance to run an effective offense. The proper spacing and collaboration among the five offensive players can force the defenders to run a longer distance to recover after a help or a double team.

SPACING AND COLLABORATION AS FUNDAMENTALS

The perimeter players must learn to mantain the proper distance between them after a dribble or a cut, and, at the same time, the inside player must move according to the dribble or cut of the perimeter players or the other inside player, in case the offense plays with two low-posts, or one low and one high .

We consider spacing and collaboration as normal team fundamentals, and, like any other fundamental, they must be constantly practiced. In this chapter, we will show different drills on spacing and collaboration, working both on the perimeter players and the inside players.

TWO GUARDS—DRIVE TOWARD DRILL

Aim

The aim of the two guards—drive toward drill to is to work on the collaboration between the two guards to create proper spacing, in this case, when the ball handler drives toward the teammate.

Equipment

- 4 balls

Personnel

- The perimeter players

FIGURE 9.1

How To Run the Drill

Form two lines of players at the guard spots, with the balls on the left line. Player 1 dribbles toward 2, who flares to the wing's spot, receives the ball from 1, and makes a jump shot, as shown in Figure 9.1.

Then, 2 goes to the end of 1's line, and 1 to the end of 2's. The drill is also run driving from the left side of the court, and ends after a certain number of shots or a set amount of time.

Details to Teach and Underline

- The teammate of the ball handler must move away immediately when he sees the ball handler driving toward him and maintain the same distance between them.

Variation

The player drives to the basket instead of making a jump shot. A defender guards 1 at 50 percent, harassing him while he is passing the ball.

169

TWO GUARDS–DRIVE AWAY DRILL

Aim

The aim of the two guards–drive away drill to is to work on the collaboration between the two guards to create proper spacing, such as when the ball handler drives away from his teammate.

Equipment

- 4 balls

Personnel

- The perimeter players

How To Run the Drill

Form two lines of players at the two-guard spots, with the balls on the left line. Player 1 dribbles to the left-wing spot, away from 2, who flashes to the high-post spot, receives from 1, and makes a jump shot, as shown in Figure 9.2.

After the shot, 2 goes to the end of 1's line, and 1 to the end of 2's. The drill is also run on the right side of the court, and ends after a certain number of shots or a set amount of time.

Details to Teach and Underline

- The teammate of the ball handler must move when he sees the ball handler driving away from him and mantain the same distance.

Variation

The player drives to the basket, instead of making a jump shot. A defender guards 1 at 50 percent, harassing him while he is passing the ball.

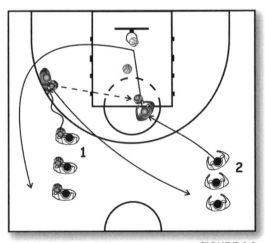

FIGURE 9.2

THREE PLAYERS–DRIVE TO THE BASELINE DRILL

Aim

The aim of the three players–drive to the baseline drill is to create the habit of maintaining spacing and collaborating, based on a teammate's drive to the baseline.

Equipment

- 3 balls

Personnel

- All the perimeter players

How to Run the Drill

The perimeter players are divided into three groups, one on the left wing, one in the middle of the half-court with three balls, and one on the right wing.

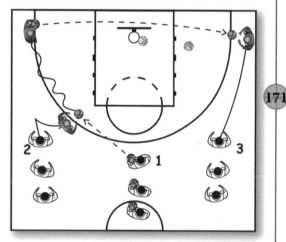

Player 1 passes to 2, who previously has made a V cut. As soon as 2 drives to the baseline, 1 gets to the left corner of the free-throw area, while 3 flares in the corner, outside the three-point line. Player 2 makes a skip pass to 3, who shoots a three-pointer, as shown in Figure 9.3.

FIGURE 9.3

This is the rotation: 1 goes to the end of 2's line, 2 to the end of 3's line, and 3 to the end of 1's line. The drill is run for a certain number of shots per player or for a set amount of time.

Details to Teach and Underline

- The three players' movements must be quick, but under control.
- Properly utilize all the fundamentals involved while running at game speed.

Variation

The ball handler 2 passes to 1 at the corner of the free-throw area. Two defenders guard 1 and 3 at 50 percent, harassing them while they passing the ball.

THREE PLAYERS—DRIVE TO THE MIDDLE DRILL

AIM

The aim of the three players—drive to the middle drill is to create the habit of spacing and collaboration, based on a teammate's drive to the lane.

Equipment

- 3 balls

Personnel

- All the perimeter players

How to Run the Drill

172

The perimeter players are divided into three groups, one on the left wing, one in the middle of the half-court with three balls, and one on the right wing.

Player 1 passes to 2, who previously has made a V cut. As soon as 2 drives to the lane, 1 flares to the right-wing spot of the free-throw area, while 3 flares in the corner, outside the three-point line. Player 2 passes to 1, who passes to 3 for a three-point shot, as shown in Figure 9.4. Player 3 can also pass back to 1 for a three-point shot.

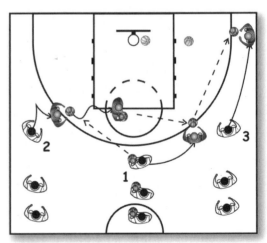

FIGURE 9.4

This is the rotation: 1 goes to the end of 2's line, 2 to the end of 3's line, and 3 to the end of 1's line. The drill is run for a certain number of shots per player or for a set amount of time.

Details to Teach and Underline

- The three players' movements must be quick, but under control.
- Properly utilize the fundamentals involved while running at game speed.

Variation

Player 3 drives to the basket, instead shooting a three-pointer. Two defenders guard 2 and 1 at 50 percent, harassing them while they are passing the ball.

THREE PLAYERS–DRIVE TO THE BASELINE–FOUR PASSES DRILL

Aim

The aim of the three players–drive to the baseline–four passes drill is to practice spacing and collaboration among three players, after driving to the baseline and making four passes before shooting.

173

Equipment

- 4 balls

Personnel

- All the perimeter players

How to Run the Drill

Divide the team into six groups, three on each half-court: two groups are aligned at the left- and right-wing spots, and one in the middle of the court, with two balls.

Player 2 makes a V cut and receives the ball from 1. Right after the pass, 1 fakes to go toward 2, then goes in the opposite direction at the right-wing spot, while 3 goes in the corner. Player 2 drives hard to the baseline and makes a skip pass to 3 in the other corner. Player 3 passes to 1, who drives to the lane and passes in the short corner to 2, who finishes with a layup or a jump shot, as shown in Figure 9.5. Player 2 can also pass to 1 for a jump shot, or to 3 for a three-point shot.

This is the rotation: 2 goes to the end of 1's line, 1 to the end of 3's line, and 3 to end of the 2's line. The drill is run for a certain number of repetitions per player, on all three positions, and is also run on the right side of the court.

FIGURE 9.5

Details to Teach and Underline

- Space and relocate as soon as the ball is moved with a pass or a drive.
- Move at game speed.
- Make crisp and strong passes.
- Make angled cuts.
- Drive aggressively to go to the basket.

174

Variation

Three defenders guard the three offensive players at 50 percent, harassing them while they are passing the ball.

THREE PLAYERS–DRIVE TO THE MIDDLE–FOUR PASSES DRILL

Aim

The aim of the three players–drive to the middle–four passes drill is to practice spacing and collaboration among three players, after driving on the baseline, and making four passes before shooting.

Equipment

- 4 balls

Personnel

- All the perimeter players

How to Run the Drill

Divide the team into six groups, three on each half-court: two groups are aligned at the left- and right-wing spots, and one in the middle of the court, with the balls.

Player 2 makes a V cut and receives the ball from 1. Right after the pass, 1 fakes to go toward 3, then comes back, while 3 goes in the corner. Player 2 drives hard to the middle of the lane and passes to 1, who passes to 3. Player 3 drives on the baseline, and passes to 2, who has moved down near the corner and finishes with a three-pointer or a layup, as shown in Figure 9.6. Player 2 can also pass to 1 for a jump shot.

FIGURE 9.6

This is the rotation: 2 goes to the end of 1's line, 1 to the end of 3's line, and 3 to end of 2's line. The drill is run for a certain number of repetitions per player, on all three positions, and is also run on the right side of the court.

Details to Teach and Underline

- Space and relocate as soon as the ball is moved with a pass or a drive.
- Move at game speed.
- Make crisp and strong passes.
- Make angled cuts.
- Drive and go to the basket aggressively.

Variation

Three defenders guard the three offensive players at 50 percent, harassing them while they are passing the ball.

THREE PLAYERS AND DRIVES-AND-KICKS DRILL

AIM

The aim of the three players-drives-and-kicks drill is to bring spacing and collaboration to a higher level, working on more driving penetrations and passing.

Equipment

- 4 balls

Personnel

- All the perimeter players

How to Run the Drill

The drill is similar to the one shown in Figure 9.5, but now the players make more penetrations, never two consecutive ones on the same side, and skip passes, so they must adjust spacing in different situations.

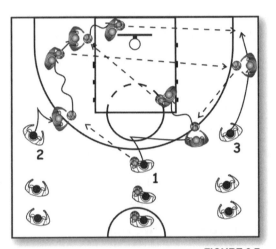

FIGURE 9.7

Divide the team into six groups, three on each half-court: two groups are aligned at the left- and right-wing spots, and one in the middle of the court, with the balls.

Player 2 makes a V cut and receives the ball from 1. Right after the pass, 1 fakes to go toward 2, then goes in the opposite direction at the wing spot, while 3 goes down. Player 2 drives hard to the baseline and makes a skip pass to 3. Player 3 passes to 1, who drives to the lane and passes to 2. Player 2 drives along the baseline and passes to 3, who has moved to the deep corner and finishes with a three-pointer or a middle-range jump shot, as shown in Figure 9.7.

This is the rotation: 2 goes to the end of 1's line, 1 to the end of 3's line, and 3 to the end of 2's line. The drill is run for a certain number of repetitions per player, on all three positions, and is also run on the right side of the court.

Details to Teach and Underline

- Space and relocate as soon as the ball is moved with a pass or a drive.
- Move at game speed.
- Make crisp and strong passes.
- Make angled cuts.
- Drive and go to the basket aggressively.

Variation

Three defenders guard the three offensive players at 50 percent, harassing them while they are passing the ball.

LOW-POST BALL SIDE–DRIVE TO THE BASELINE DRILL

Aim

The aim of the low-post ball side–drive to the baseline drill is to work on spacing and relocating on a drive to the baseline with three perimeter players and one inside player on the ball side.

Equipment

- 3 balls

Personnel

- The entire team

How to Run the Drill

The perimeter players are divided into three groups, one on the left wing, one in the middle of the half-court with two balls, and one on the right wing, while the inside players are set outside of the baseline, with one of them on the low-post spot.

Player 1 passes to 3, who previously has made a V cut. As soon as 3 drives to the baseline, 1 relocates to 3's wing spot, while 2 flares in the opposite corner, outside the three-point line, and 5 goes to the high-post spot, at the corner the free-throw area on the ball side. Player 3 can pass to 5 for a jump shot or a drive to the basket, or to 2 or 1 for a three-pointer, as shown in Figure 9.8.

FIGURE 9.8

This is the rotation: 1 goes to the end of 2's line, 2, to the end of 3's line, and 3 to the end of 1's line, while 5 goes to the end of the inside players' line. The drill is run for a certain number of repetitions, or a set amount of time, and is also run on the right side of the court.

Variation

Three defenders guard the three offensive players at 50 percent, harassing them while they are passing the ball.

LOW-POST BALL SIDE–DRIVE TO THE MIDDLE DRILL

Aim

The aim of the low-post ball side–drive to the middle drill is to work on spacing and relocating on a drive-to-the-middle penetration, with three perimeter players and one inside player on the ball side.

Equipment
- 3 balls

Personnel
- The entire team

How to Run the Drill

The perimeter players are divided into three groups, one on the left wing, one in the middle of the half-court with two balls, and one on the right wing, while the inside players are set outside the baseline, with one of them on the low-post spot.

Player 1 passes to 3, who previously has made a V cut. As soon as 3 drives to middle of the lane, 2 goes to the opposite corner, 1 relocates to 2's wing spot, while 5 pops out in the short-corner spot. Player 3 can pass to 5 for a jump shot or a drive to the basket, or to 2 or 1 for a three-point shot, as shown in Figure 9.9.

This is the rotation: 1 goes to the end of 2's line, 2, to the end of 3's line, and 3 to the end of 1's line, while 5 goes to the end of the inside players' line. The drill is run for a certain number of repetitions or a set amount of time, and is also run on the right side of the court.

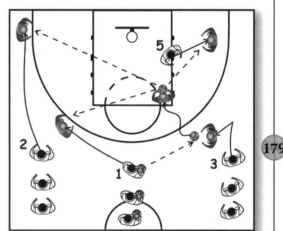

FIGURE 9.9

Variation

Two defenders guard 1 and 3 at 50 percent, harassing them while they are passing the ball.

LOW-POST HELP SIDE–DRIVE TO THE MIDDLE DRILL
Aim

The aim of the low-post help side–drive to the middle drill is to work on spacing and relocating on a drive-to-the-middle penetration, with three perimeter players and one inside player on the help side.

Equipment
- 3 balls

Personnel

■ The entire team

How to Run the Drill

The perimeter players are divided into three groups, one on the left wing, one in the middle of the half-court with two balls, and one on the right wing, while the inside players are set outside the baseline, with one of them on the low-post spot on the help side.

FIGURE 9.10

Player 1 passes to 3, who previously has made a V cut. As soon as 3 drives to the middle of the lane, 2 goes to the opposite corner and 1 relocates to 2's wing spot, while 5 cuts in the lane and posts up on the ball-side low-post spot. Player 3 can pass to 5 for a jump shot or a drive to the basket, or to 2 or 1 for a three-pointer, as shown in Figure 9.10.

This is the rotation: 1 goes to the end of 2's line, 2 to the end of 3's line, and 3 to the end of 1's line, while 5 goes to the end of the inside players' line. The drill is run for a certain number of repetitions, or a set amount of time, and is also run on the right side of the court.

Variation

Two defenders guard 1 and 3 at 50 percent, harassing them while they are passing the ball.

LOW-POST HELP SIDE–DRIVE TO THE BASELINE DRILL

Aim

The aim of the low-post help side–drive to the baseline drill is to work on spacing and relocating on a drive to the baseline, with three perimeter players and one inside player on the help side.

Equipment
- 3 balls

Personnel
- The entire team

How to Run the Drill

The perimeter players are divided in three groups, one on the left wing, one in the middle of the half-court with two balls, and one on the right wing, while the inside players are set outside of baseline, with one of them on the low-post spot on the help side.

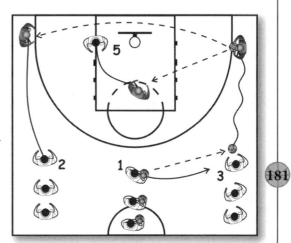

FIGURE 9.11

Player 1 passes to 3, who previously has made a V cut. As soon as 3 drives to the baseline, 2 goes to the opposite corner and 1 relocates to the 3's wing spot, while 5 cuts in middle of the lane. Player 3 can pass to 5 for a jump shot or a layup, or to 2 or 1 for a three-pointer, as shown in Figure 9.11.

This is the rotation: 1 goes to the end of 2's line, 2 to the end of 3's line, and 3 to the end of 1's line, while 5 goes to the end of the inside players' line. The drill is run for a certain number of repetitions or a set amount of time, and is also run on the right side of the court.

Variation

Two defenders guard 1 and 3 at 50 percent, harassing them while they are passing the ball.

INSIDE PLAYERS' COLLABORATION–DRIVE TO THE BASELINE DRILL

Aim

The aim of the inside players' collaboration–drive to the baseline drill is to get the perimeter and inside players accustomed to working together after a baseline drive.

Equipment

- 4 balls

Personnel

- The entire team

How to Run the the Drill

The team is divided into three groups, one group of inside players on the left wing, one group of perimeter players in the middle of the court with the balls, and the other group of perimeter players on the right-wing spot.

FIGURE 9.12

Player 5 cuts in the lane and posts up. At the same time, 1 passes to 3, who drives to the baseline, while 1 replaces 5. Player 3 finds the proper passing angle and gets the ball to 5, who goes to the basket, as shown in Figure 9.12.

Then another group of three players steps in. The same three players run the drill five times on the right side and five times on the left.

Details to Teach and Underline

- Make an accurate pass to the target offered by the inside player.

Variation

The inside player makes a skip pass to the opposite wing, who shoots a three-

182

pointer. Two defenders guard 1 and 3 at 50 percent, harassing them while they are passing the ball.

INSIDE PLAYERS' COLLABORATION–WING DRIVE DRILL

AIM

The aim of the inside players' collaboration–wing drive drill is for the perimeter and inside players to get accustomed to work together after a drive to the wing.

Equipment

- 4 balls

Personnel

- The entire team

How to Run the the Drill

The team is divided into three groups, one group of inside players on the left wing, one group of perimeter players in the middle of the court with the balls, and the other group of perimeter players on the right-wing spot.

183

Player 5 cuts in the lane and posts up. At the same time, 1 drives toward 3, who cuts to the corner and receives the ball from 1. Player 3 finds the proper passing

FIGURE 9.13

angle and gets the ball to 5, who goes to the basket, as shown in Figure 9.13.

Then another group of three players steps in. The same three players run the drill five times on the right side and five times on the left.

Details to Teach and Underline

- Make an accurate pass to the target offered by the inside player.

Variation

The inside player makes a skip pass to the ball-side wing, who shoots a three-pointer. Two defenders guard 1 and 3 at 50 percent, harassing them while they are passing the ball.

PERIMETER PLAYERS' POST UP–WING DRIVE DRILL

Aim

The aim of the perimeter players' post up–wing drive drill is to get the perimeter players accustomed to post up and work together with the inside players, after a drive to the wing.

Equipment

- 4 balls

Personnel

- The entire team

184

How to Run the the Drill

The team is divided into three groups, one group of inside players on the left wing, one group of perimeter players in the middle of the court with the balls, and the other group of perimeter players on the right-wing spot.

FIGURE 9.14

Player 5 cuts in the lane, and goes out in the opposite corner. At the same time, 1 drives toward 3, who relocates to the low-post area and posts up. Player 5 receives the ball from 1, and gets the ball to 3, who goes to the basket, as shown in Figure 9.14.

Then another group of three players steps in. The same three players run the drill five times on the right side and five times on the left.

Details to Teach and Underline

- Make an accurate pass to the target offered by the inside player.

Variation

The inside player makes a pass to the ball-side wing, who shoots a three-pointer. Two defenders guard 1 and 5 at 50 percent, harassing them while they are passing the ball.

HIGH-POST-BACKDOOR DRILL

Aim

The aim of the high-post-backdoor drill is to work on the collaboration and spacing between the perimeter and the inside players on a high-backdoor play.

Equipment

- 4 balls

Personnel

- The entire team

How to Run the the Drill

The team is divided into three groups, one group of inside players on the left wing, one group of perimeter players in the middle of the court with the balls, and the other group of perimeter players on the right-wing spot.

While 1 drives to the wing 3, 5 makes a flash-cut to the free-throw area and receives the ball from 1. Player 3 makes a backdoor cut to the basket as soon as 5 has received the ball; then he receives

FIGURE 9.15

from 5, finishing with a layup, as shown in Figure 9.15.

Then another group of three players steps in. The same three players run the drill five times on the right side and five times on the left.

Details to Teach and Underline
- Time the cut of the wing, as soon as the high post has received the ball.
- Make an accurate pass to the target offered by the inside player.

Variation
The inside player makes a pass to the ball-side wing, who shoots a three-pointer. Two defenders guard 1 and 5 at 50 percent, harassing them while they are passing the ball.

CUT AND POST DOWN LOW WITH DEFENSE DRILL

Aim

186

The aim of the cut and post down low with defense drill is to practice spacing and collaboration between the inside and outside players under game situations.

Equipment
- 4 balls

Personnel
- The entire team

How to Run the the Drill
The team is divided into three groups, one group of inside players on the left wing, one group of perimeter players in the middle of the court with the balls, and the other group of perimeter players on the right-wing spot. The two

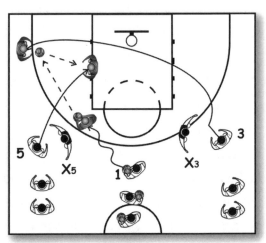

FIGURE 9.16

players on the wing are guarded by two defenders.

Player 1 cannot pass to 5, but he wants to give him the ball, so he drives toward him, and at the same time 3 cuts and goes to the corner on the ball side. Player 5 coordinates his cut and posts down low; 1 passes the ball to 3, and 3 to 5, who makes a power shot, a layup or another type of shot as shown in Figure 9.16. Then another three players step in. The same three players run the drill five times on the right side and five on the left.

Details to Teach and Underline
- The timing of the cuts and the passes must be accurate.
- Make an accurate pass to the target offered by the inside player.

Variation
The inside player on the low-post makes a pass the perimeter player at the guard spot, who makes a three-pointer.

HIGH-POST-BACKDOOR CUT WITH THE DEFENSE DRILL
Aim
The aim of the high-post-backdoor cut with defense drill is to practice spacing and collaboration between the inside and outside players under game situations, working particularly on the backdoor cut of the inside players.

Equipment
- 4 balls

Personnel
- The entire team

How to Run the the Drill
The team is divided into three groups, one group of inside players on the left wing, one group of perimeter players in the middle of the court with the balls,

187

and the other group of perimeter play-ers on the right-wing spot. The two players on the wing are guarded by two defenders.

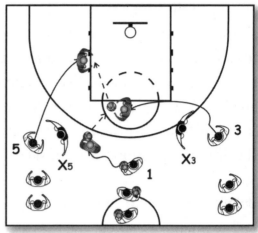

FIGURE 9.17

Player 1 cannot pass to 5, but he wants to give him the ball, so he drives toward him, and at the same time 3 cuts and goes to the free-throw area on the ball side. Player 5 coordinates his backdoor cut, 1 passes the ball to 3, 2 times his backdoor cut, and 3 passes to 5, who goes to the basket, as shown in Figure 9.17.

Then another three players step in. The same three players run the drill five times on the right side and five on the left.

Details to Teach and Underline
- The timing of the cuts and the passes must be accurate.
- Make an accurate pass, preferably a bounce pass, to the player, who makes the backdoor cut.

Variation
The player on high post makes a pass to the perimeter player at the guard spot, who makes a three-pointer.

HIGH- AND LOW-POST COLLABORATION SERIES
Getting the ball near the basket gives the offense the chance to get a higher percentage of shots. If the high- and low-post players are able to play together, this offers more possibilities to score and more options to the inside players. The following are simple drills to practice this collective fundamental.

LOW-POST DRIVE DRILL

Aim

The aim of the low-post drive drill is to get the inside players accustomed to coordinating their movements based on the drive of one of them.

Equipment

- 2 balls

Personnel

- All the inside players
- Two passers
- One coach

How to Run the Drill

The inside players are behind the baseline, and two of them are set at the two low-post spots, at the left and right sides of the three-second lane. Two passers are at the wing spots, at the left and right sides near the three-point line, and one coach is in the middle of the court.

The coach shouts, "Left (or right) baseline," or "Left (or right) middle." The passer on the left side, in this case, will

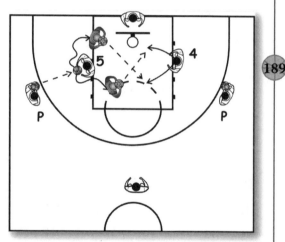

FIGURE 9.18

pass the ball to 5, who will turn and drive in the direction called by the coach, and 4 will move in the opposite direction, as shown in Figure 9.18.

On the baseline drive, 4 will cut in the middle of the lane, receive, and shoot. On the middle drive, he will cut on the baseline, receive, and shoot. The player gets the rebound, passes the ball back outside, and again runs the drill, basing his moves on the calls of the coach. The drill is run for a certain number of shots per player or a set amount of time.

189

Details to Teach and Underline

- Make the moves at game speed.
- Stay low throughout the drill in order to explode to the basket.

Variation

Two defenders are added, covering the two inside players at 50 percent at the beginning, and then aggressively.

HIGH-LOW POST-MOTION DRILL

The aim of the high-low post-motion drill is to get players accustomed to a high and a low-post to coordinate their movements.

Equipment

- 2 balls

Personnel

- All the inside players
- Two passers
- One coach

How to Run the Drill

The inside players are behind the base-line, and two of them are set at the two low-post spots, at the left and right sides of the three-second lane. Two passers are at the wing spots, at the left and right sides near the three-point line, and one coach is in the middle of the court.

The coach calls the name of the player, who runs at the high-post spot

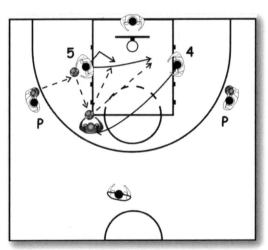

FIGURE 9.19

on the same side of the other low-post, and then shouts, "Middle" or "Baseline." The passer, in this case, will pass the ball to 5, who will pass to 4, as shown in Figure 9.19. Then 5 will fake in the opposite direction and cut in the middle of the lane, or cut along the baseline, receive the ball, and shoot.

The player gets the rebound, passes the ball back outside, and again runs the drill, basing his moves on the calls of the coach. The drill is run for a certain number of shots per players or a set amount of time.

Details to Teach and Underline
- Make the moves at game speed.
- Stay low throughout the drill in order to explode to the basket.

Variation
Two defenders are added, covering the two inside players at 50 percent at the beginning, and then aggressively.

HIGH-LOW POST-BASELINE DRIVE DRILL
The aim of the high-low post-baseline drive drill is to get the inside players accustomed to coordinating their movements when the high-post drives baseline.

Equipment
- 2 balls

Personnel
- All the inside players
- Two passers
- One coach

How to Run the Drill
The inside players are behind the baseline, and two of them are set at the two low-post spots, at the left and right sides of the three-second lane. Two passers are at

the wing spots, at the left and right sides near the three-point line, and one coach is in the middle of the court.

The coach calls the name of the player, who runs at the high-post spot on the same side of the low-post and then shouts, "Baseline." The passer, in this case, will pass the ball to 4, as shown in Figure 9.20a. Then, 4 drives baseline, while 5 goes opposite along the baseline, receives the ball from 4, and shoots.

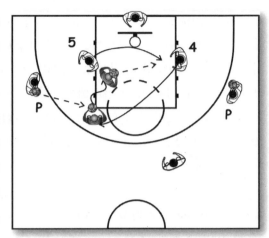

FIGURE 9.20a

If the coach shouts, "Middle," 4 will drive in the middle of the lane, while 5 will go behind him on the opposite side, receive, and shoot, as shown in Figure 9.20b.

The players get the rebound, pass the ball back outside, and again run the drill, basing their moves on the calls of the coach. The drill is run for a certain number of shots per player or a set amount of time.

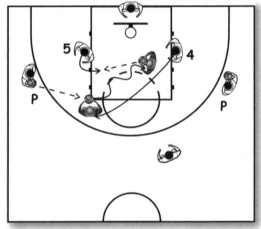

FIGURE 9.20b

Details to Teach and Underline

- Make the moves at game speed.
- Stay low throughout the drill in order to explode to the basket.

Variation

Two defenders are added, covering the two inside players at 50 percent at the beginning, and then aggressively.

192

10
Fast Break Drills

Running is essential to the game of basketball. Players enjoy running the fast break, making a no-look pass, an alley hoop for a dunk, or an open three-point shot to end the fast break. The crowd gets excited by a team that runs in every possible situation, such as after a defensive rebound, a steal, or an out-of bounds shot.

Playing a fast-break style of basketball is not easy. Recognition, speed, ball-handling skills, and decision making are critical to the success of a fast break. The players must have simple but consistent rules, know how to act or react in different defensive situations, and know which lanes to occupy on the court.

Players must practice so they can move the ball up the court and into scoring position as fast as possible, so that the defense is outnumbered and doesn't have time to set up. If not performed properly, the fast break could become a stampede of crazy broncos.

In this chapter, we will show different drills that can help to build an aggressive and efficient fast break, from a two-on-one to a five-on-four.

Passing, especially while running at full speed, and making the right decision as to whom to pass the ball to in order to score an easy basket are the basic elements of the fast break. Scoring an uncontested basket is a big thrill for the offense and upsetting to the defense, not to mention a headache for the rival coach.

ONE-ON-ZERO DRILL

Aim

The aim of the one-on-zero drill is to practice a long pass, receive while running, and score.

Equipment

- 2 balls

Personnel

- The entire team

194

How to Run the Drill

The team is divided into groups of three players each: one player with the ball is under the basket, one on the left wing, and one 6 feet away from the mid-court line, on the opposite half-court.

Player 1 tosses the ball on the backboard, gets the rebound, and passes the ball to 2, who has previously made a V cut. Player 2 drives sideline and goes to the basket, while 3, as soon as 2 has crossed the mid-court line, touches the mid-court line, and sprints to get the rebound of 2's shot. Right after the pass to 2, 1 sprints to the opposite basket until he reaches the right side of the court at the free-throw line extension. Then, he sprints back to the basket from where he started the drill, receives the ball from 3, and scores a layup, as shown in Figure 10.1.

Then, another group of three players steps in. This is the rotation: 2 goes to 3's spot, 3 to 1's spot, and 1 to 2's spot. The drill is also run on the right side of the court. The drill ends after a certain number of scored basket or after a set amount of time.

Details to Teach and Underline

- Use a speed-dribble to drive to the basket, making as few dribbles as possible.
- The receiver of the long pass must sprint as close as possible to the sideline, in order to give the passer a good passing angle.
- Make the long pass ahead of the running teammate.
- Go toward the ball with both hands.
- Do not watch the ball at the last second before receiving it; watch it some seconds before.

Variation

Add two defenders, who follow the offensive players, playing defense at 50 percent and harassing the passers while they are passing the ball.

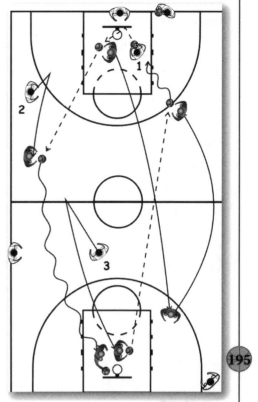

FIGURE 10.1

ONE-CHAIR–LONG-PASS DRILL

Aim

The aim of the one-chair–long-pass drill is to get the players used to making long passes, receiving while running, and scoring.

Equipment

- 3 balls
- 1 chair

Personnel

- The entire team

195

How to Run the Drill

The team is divided into groups of three players, set near and along the baseline, with one player in the left corner, one under the basket with the ball, and one in the right corner. One chair is set at the left corner of the free-throw area, on the other half-court.

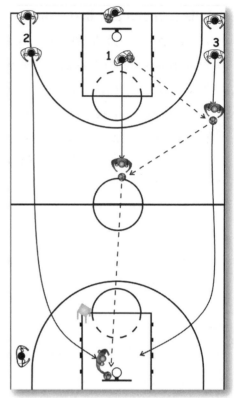

FIGURE 10.2a

Player 1 passes the ball to 3, then sprints down the middle of the court in a straight line to the opposite basket. At the same time, 2 sprints along the left sideline to the opposite basket.

Player 1 receives the ball back from 3, who also, after the pass, sprints near the right sideline. Both 2 and 3 cut to the basket at the free-throw line extension. Player 1 makes a long pass to 2, who drives to the basket and finishes with a layup, as shown in Figure 10.2a.

Player 1, who has sprinted to the opposite basket right after the pass to 2, circles around the chair, and goes back to where he started the drill. After the layup, 2 goes on the wing spot on the right side, while 3 gets the ball, goes out-of-bounds, and makes an outlet pass to 2, who makes a long pass to 1, who finishes with a layup, as shown in Figure 10.2b.

Then three other players step in. Each player in each group circles around the chair, receives a long pass, and finishes with a layup. The drill is run also on the right side of the court and ends after a certain number of shots or a set amount of time.

Details to Teach and Underline

- All passes must be accurate.
- Make the long pass ahead of the running teammate.
- Go toward the ball with both hands.
- Do not watch the ball at the last second before receiving it, but rather some seconds before.

Variation

Add two defenders, who follow the passers, playing defense at 50 percent, and harassing the passers while they are passing the ball.

TWO-ON-TWO STANDING DEFENDERS DRILL

Aim

FIGURE 10.2b

The aim of the two-on-two standing defenders drill is to work on passing while running, while two standing defenders try to steal or deflect the passes.

Equipment

- 1 ball

Personnel

- The entire team

How to Run the Drill

The team is divided into two groups of six players each: two players with one ball are set at the low corners of the three-second lane near the baseline, one player outside the baseline, one player at the mid-court line extension, and two players, one at the jump-ball area and one at the free-throw area, facing the opposite basket.

Players 1 and 2 pass the ball to each other, keeping the same spacing, while players 3 and 4 act as standing defenders and try to steal or deflect the passes. As soon as 1 and 2 have ended the fast break with a layup, 4 gets the ball and makes an outlet pass to 3. These two players go on fast break against 5 and 06, who have stepped on the court at the jump-ball area and the free-throw area, respectively, and act as standing defenders, as shown in Figure 10.3.

After all six players have performed the drill for a certain number of scored baskets or for a set amount of time, six other players step in.

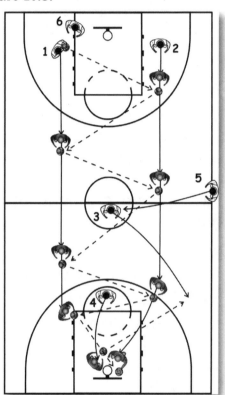

FIGURE 10.3

Details to Teach and Underline

- Use head and ball fakes to get the defenders off balance before passing.
- No fancy passes.
- No dribbling.
- Teach the defenders to make defensive fakes to harass the offensive players as much as possible.

TWO-ON-ONE DRILL

Aim

The aim of the two-on-one drill is to work on a two-player fast break to teach proper spacing and scoring solutions.

Equipment

- 4 balls

Personnel

- The entire team

198

How to Run the Drill

The team is divided into four groups of three players each. Each group has two offensive players at the sides of the three-second lane and one defensive player at the free-throw line with the ball, while the other groups are set outside the two baselines.

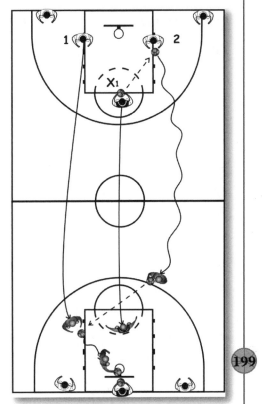

FIGURE 10.4

The player with the ball, X, passes it to 2, then sprints back on defense, while 1 and 2 sprint to the opposite basket on the fast break, as shown in Figure 10.4.

If the defender steals the ball or gets the rebound of a missed basket, he goes on offense against the two offensive players, who become defenders. Three new players step in after a scored basket. The drill ends after a certain number of scored baskets, or after a set amount of time.

199

Details to Teach and Underline

- Keep proper spacing between the two offensive players.
- No fancy passes.
- Once he reaches the free-throw line extension, the ball handler must go straight to the basket, passing to his teammate only if the defender blocks the path to the basket.
- Both offensive players, as well as the defensive player, go for the rebound.
- Teach the defender to make defensive fakes to harass the offensive players as much as possible.

TWO-ON-ONE WITH A TRAILER DRILL

AIM

The aim of the two-on-one with a trailer drill is to work on the fast break with two players to teach proper spacing and scoring solutions and to beat the defender before the arrival of the defensive trailer.

Equipment

- 4 balls

Personnel

- The entire team

How to Run the Drill

The team is divided into four groups, two outside one baseline and two outside the opposite baseline. Each group has two offensive players at the sides of the three-second lane, one defensive player at the free-throw line, with the ball, and one defensive player outside the baseline,

The player with the ball, X1, passes it to 2, and then runs back on defense, while 1 and 2 sprint to the opposite basket on the fast break. As soon as 2 has received the ball, X2, the trailer, recovers as quickly as possible, sprinting to the opposite basket, as shown in Figure 10.5.

Player 1 or 2 must score before the arrival of X2. The drill ends after a scored basket by offensive player 1 or 2 or if defenders X1 and X2 get the ball on a steal or a defensive rebound, become the offensive players, and try to score against 1 and 2.

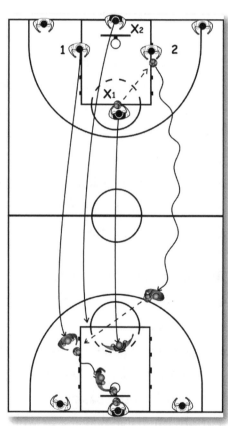

FIGURE 10.5

After a scored basket by this group, another group steps in. The drill ends after a certain number of scored baskets or after a set amount of time.

Details to Teach and Underline

- Keep proper spacing between the two offensive players.
- No fancy passes.
- Once the ball handler reaches the free-throw-line extension, he must go straight to the basket and pass to a teammate only if the defender blocks the path to the basket.
- Both offensive and defensive players go for the rebound.
- Teach the defenders to make defensive fakes to harass the offensive players as much as possible.

FIFTY BASKETS DRILL

Aim

The aim of the fifty baskets drill is to practice shooting on a fast break under stress and fatigue.

Equipment

- 1 ball for every player

Personnel

- The entire team
- A coach

How to Run the Drill

The team is lined up on the left side of the court at the wing-spot position, each player with a ball, and the drill starts with a player with the ball under the basket. A coach stands outside the court at the extension of the mid-court line.

The player under the basket tosses the ball on the backboard, gets the rebound, and makes an outlet pass, in this case, to the first player on the left-wing line, who has made a V cut before receiving the ball. The receiver of the pass dribbles in the middle of the court, while the rebounder sprints along the left sideline, cuts to the basket at the free-throw line extension, and receives the ball, finishing with a layup.

The passer goes to the rebound, grabs the ball before it hits the floor, and passes to a teammate, who shoots the ball. They repeat the pattern on the other side of the floor, as shown in Figure 10.6. The drill ends after 3 minutes.

The players must score fifty baskets in 3 minutes. The coach keeps a record of the missed baskets, as well as of how many baskets are still needed to reach the fifty-scored-baskets mark, if the times expires.

The entire team runs one sprint for every missed basket and one sprint for every basket still needed to reach the fifty baskets mark.

FIGURE 10.6

Details to Teach and Underline

- The ball handler must speed-dribble, making as few dribbles as possible to go to the opposite basket.
- Make a quick and accurate outlet pass every time.

THREE PLAYERS CIRCLE DRILL

Aim

The aim of the three players circle drill is to practice how to immediately occupy the three lanes for a three-player fast break.

Equipment

- 2 balls

Personnel

- The entire team
- A coach

How to Run the Drill

The team is divided into four groups of three players each. The first group is set around the free-throw circle, and the coach is under the basket with a ball.

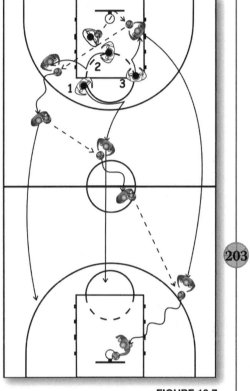

The three players run clockwise around the free-throw circle. When the coach shouts "Go," he tosses the ball on the backboard. The nearest player, 3, grabs the rebound and yells "Ball," while 2 sprints on the left-wing spot, yelling "Left," and receives from 3. At the same time, 1 sprints in the middle lane of the court, yelling "Middle," and receives from 2, while 3, after he has passed the ball to 2, sprints to occupy

FIGURE 10.7

the right lane of the court. Player 1 speed-dribbles to the opposing basket and passes the ball to 3, who finishes with a layup, as shown in Figure 10.7.

The next three players step in and run the same pattern. The drill ends after a certain number of fast breaks or after a set amount of time.

Details to Teach and Underline

- Communication is basic.
- Speed-dribble to bring the ball quickly to the offensive half-court.
- Make only two, or maximum three, dribbles before passing ahead.

Variation

Two defenders are added, set outside mid-court line. They run on the court as soon as the outlet pass is made and play defense.

FIVE PLAYERS CIRCLE DRILL

Aim

The aim of the five players circle drill is to practice immediately occupying the five lanes for a five-player fast break.

Equipment

- 1 balls

Personnel

- The entire team
- A coach

How to Run the Drill

The team is divided into two groups of five players each. The first group is set around the free-throw circle, and the coach is under the basket with a ball.

The five players run clockwise around the free-throw circle. When the coach shouts "Go," he tosses the ball on the backboard. The nearest player, 3, grabs the rebound, yells "Ball," and passes to right or left wing: now all five players must occupy the five fast-break lanes, the two lateral wings' lanes, the central lane, and the first and second trailers' lanes, calling out which lane they are occupying.

FIGURE 10.8

The ball handler passes the ball to one of his teammates, who shoots a middle-range jump shot, a three-pointer, or a layup, as shown in Figure 10.8. The same five players get the rebound and run the fast break on the other basket, and so on until all five players have made a shot. Then the other five players step into the court.

Details to Teach and Underline

- Communication is basic.
- Speed-dribble to bring the ball quickly to the offensive half-court.
- Run in each called lane.

Variation

Three or four defenders are added and set outside the mid-court line. They run on the court, as soon as the outlet pass is made and play four-on-five.

THREE SHOTS FAST BREAK DRILL

Aim

The aim of the three shots fast break drill is to get the players accustomed to shooting off the fast break.

Equipment

- 5 balls

Personnel

- The entire team
- Two coaches

How to Run the Drill

The team is divided into groups of three players. The first group steps into the court: one player is under the basket with the ball, and the other two are in the left and right corners, while two coaches with one ball each, are set outside the opposite baseline on the other half-court.

The first three players make a passing wave, then, when they reach the three-point line, 2 drives to the basket, finishing with a layup, while 1 and 3, who have stopped outside the three-point line, receive the balls from the coaches and make three-pointers, as shown in Figure 10.9a.

The two outside shooters, 1 and 3, get the rebounds of their own shots and pass the balls to the coaches, while the player in the middle lane, 2, who has finished with a layup, gets the ball, and makes an outlet pass to one of the wings, 1, and then the players run the same pattern, going to the other basket, as shown in Figure 10.9b.

After shooting at the other basket, these three players step out of the court, and another three players step in. The drill ends after a certain number of baskets, or after a set amount of time.

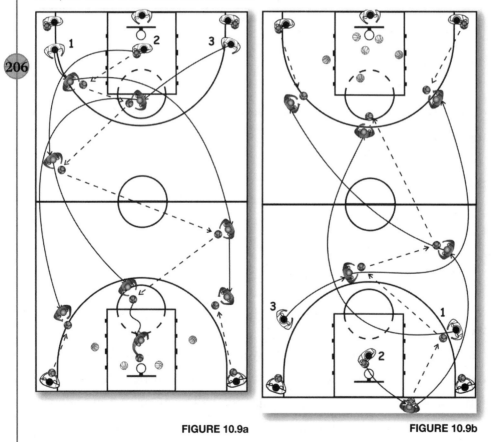

FIGURE 10.9a   **FIGURE 10.9b**

Details to Teach and Underline

- Bend the knees more in order to get better strength in the legs while making a one- or two-count stop for a three-pointer.
- Shoot as if under game conditions.

Variation

Add three defenders on each half-court to contest the three-shooters at 50 percent.

CALL-THE-DEFENSE DRILL

Aim

The aim of call-the-defense drill is to practice the fast break and the quick transition and reaction of the offensive and defensive players.

Equipment

- 2 balls

Personnel

- The entire team
- A coach

How to Run the Drill

The team is divided into two groups of five players, one set outside and along one baseline and the second one on the opposite baseline, with one ball per group, while the coach is outside the court near the mid-court line.

The players are numbered from 1 to 5. The coach calls a two-digit number, such as 25, so player 2 and player 5 run on defense, while players 1, 3, and 4 are on offense and play three-on-two fast break, as shown in Figure 10.10a.

Then the shooter, in this case 1 (or the offensive player, who has lost the ball), becomes the defender, and 2 and 5 go on offense and play two-on-one at the opposite basket, as shown in Figure 10.10b.

They step out of the court only when a basket is scored, either by the one of two offensive players, or by the defender, who either gets the rebound of the missed shot or steals the ball and goes on fast break one-on-one against the shooter or the player who made the wrong pass.

Then the other group runs the drill. The drill ends after a certain number of baskets, or after a set amount of time.

Details to Teach and Underline

- Find the most effective shooting solution, with the highest possible percentage; do not shoot just to shoot.
- All the offensive and defensive players must fight for the rebound.

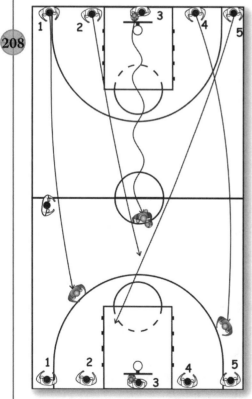

FIGURE 10.10a

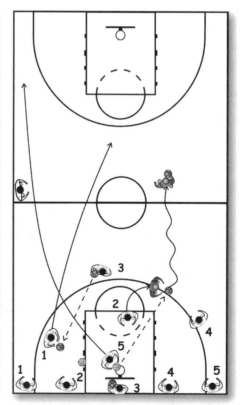

FIGURE 10.10b

- Use a speed-dribble, with as few dribbles as possible, to bring the ball on offense.
- Make sharp and crisp passes.
- On the three-on-two fast break, the ball handler stops outside the three-point line, while the two wings cut to the lane when they reach the free-throw line extension.
- Teach the defenders to make defensive fakes to harass the offensive players as much as possible.

Variation

The passer, instead of the shooter, goes on defense on the two-on-one fast break.

FOUR-ON-TWO WITH TWO TRAILERS DRILL

Aim

The aim of the four-on-two with two trailers drill is to practice the four-on-two fast break, and to teach the players to recognize immediately the proper scoring solutions when they outnumber the defense.

Equipment

- 1 ball

Personnel

- The entire team

How to Run the Drill

Form three groups of four players each. Group A, set 5 feet from the mid-court line, with one ball, is on offense against two defenders of group B in one half-court, while two players of group C act as defenders on the opposite half-court. The other players of groups B and C stand at the left and right sides of the mid-court line, outside of the court.

Group A goes on offense against the two defenders of group B, and, when they have crossed the mid-court line, the other two players of group B step on the court, sprint to the jump-ball area, and then recover on defense. Once the offense has scored the basket, or the defense has possession of the ball, group B runs the fast break against the two defenders of group C, running the same pattern, as shown in Figure 10.11. The drill ends after a certain number of baskets or after a set amount of time.

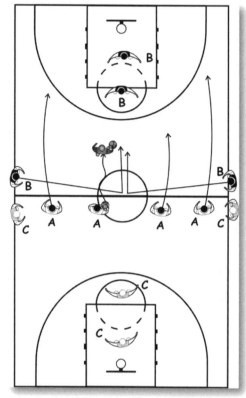

FIGURE 10.11

Details to Teach and Underline

- Do not rush the shot; choose the best and highest shooting percentage solution.

210

- All the offensive and defensive players must fight for the rebound.
- Use a speed-dribble, with as few dribbles as possible, to bring the ball on offense.
- Make sharp and crisp passes.
- Teach the defenders to make defensive fakes to harass the offensive players as much as possible.

FIVE-ON-THREE WITH TWO TRAILERS DRILL

Aim

The aim of the five-on-three with two trailers drill is to help the players to react immediately to new offensive and defensive situations, working on the transition.

Equipment

- 1 ball

Personnel

- The entire team
- A coach

How to Run the Drill

The team is divided into two groups of five offensive and five defensive players. The offensive players are set outside and along the baseline, while the defenders are aligned at the extension of the free-throw line, facing the offensive players. A coach with a ball is outside the court, near the corner.

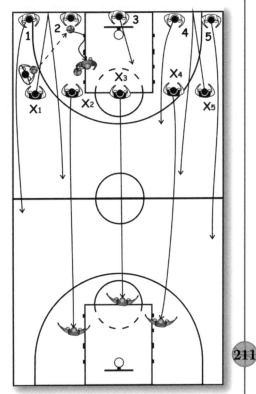

FIGURE 10.12a

The coach passes the ball to offensive player 2. As soon as the ball leaves the hands of the coach, the two defensive players near the left and right sidelines, X1 and X5, sprint to the baseline and touch it, while the other three defenders sprint on defense.

Players 1, 2, 3, 4, and 5 play five-on-three versus X2, X3, and X4, who must try to stop the offense from scoring, while the trailers, X1 and X5, recover, as shown in Figure 10.12a.

If the offense does not score while outnumbering the defense, they play five-on-five. If the defense gets the ball on a steal or a rebound of a missed shot, they run on offense, and the offensive players run on defense.

Assuming that 1 attempts the shot and that the five defenders get the ball, either from a rebound, a steal, or an out-of-bounds pass after a scored basket, they run the fast break five-on-four, while the shooter, 1, goes out of the court, as shown in Figure 10.12b. The drill ends after a certain number of baskets or after a set amount of time.

211

Details to Teach and Underline

- Find the most effective shooting solution with the highest possible percentage; do not shoot just to shoot.
- All the offensive and defensive players must fight for the rebound.
- Use a speed-dribble, with as few dribbles as possible, to bring the ball on offense.
- Make sharp and crisp passes.
- Teach the defenders to make defensive fakes to harass the offensive players as much as possible.

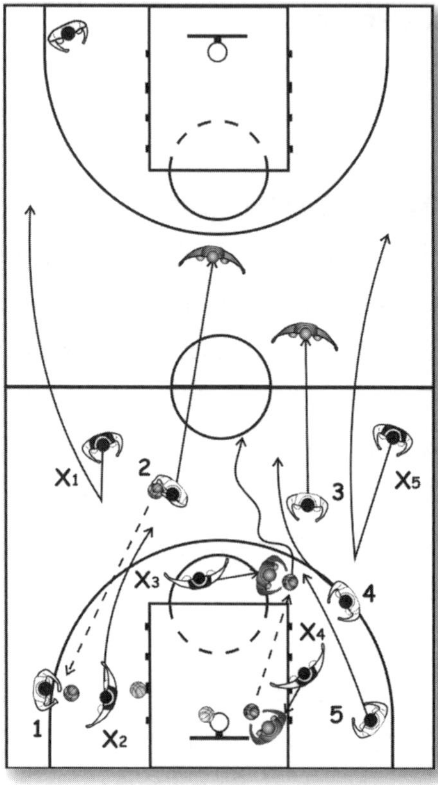

Variation

The last passer, instead of the shooter, goes out of the court on the five-on-four fast break.

FIGURE 10.12b

FIVE-PLAYER WAVE–ONE-ON-ONE DRILL

Aim

The aim of the five-player wave–one-on-one drill is to work on two fast-break situations, a three-on-two and a two-on-one, ending with a one-on-one.

Equipment

- 1 ball

Personnel

- The entire team

How to Run the Drill

The team is divided into two groups of five players each, one inside the court along the baseline and the other outside the baseline.

Players are set two in the corners, two a couple of feet away from the low corners of the three-second lane, and one with the ball under the basket.

Five-Player Wave: They start the drill making a passing wave, that is, each player passes the ball and follows the pass, going behind his teammate, who has received the ball, until all five players reach the other basket, finishing with a layup, as shown in Figure 10.13a.

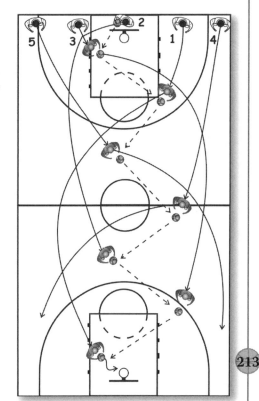

Details to Teach and Underline

- No dribbling is allowed.
- If a player dribbles, loses control of the ball, or makes a wrong pass, the group starts the passing wave again.

FIGURE 10.13a

213

Three-on-Two: Once the basket is scored, the passer and the shooter run on defense. One of the players gets the rebound if the shot is missed, or makes the inbound pass, yelling "Ball," and passing to 4, who will yell "Middle."

In this way 4 gives the other two teammates a clear signal that he will be the ball handler, dribbling in the middle of the court, while the other two offensive players call out which lanes they will occupy, 2 the left lane and 3 the right, in this case. Players 4, 2, and 3 will play against the defenders, 1 and 5, as shown in Figure 10.13.b.

Details to Teach and Underline

- Keep proper spacing between the three offensive players.

- The two wings must go on the fast break, running in the lanes nearest the sidelines, with the ball handler in the middle lane of the court (or laterally, based on the type of fast break run in the game).
- No fancy passes.
- Once he is near the three-point lane, the ball handler must stop, keeping the dribble alive, and evaluate the best passing and shooting solution, while the two wings cut to the three-second lane when they reach the free-throw line extension.
- Teach the defenders to make defensive fakes to harass the offensive players as much as possible .
- All five players involved go for the rebound.

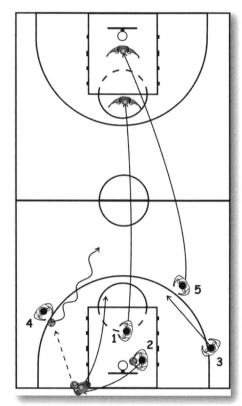

FIGURE 10.13b

Two-on-One: Let's assume that 2 has shot either a jump shot or a layup. He will then become the defender, while 1 gets the rebound, or, if the basket is scored, makes the inbound pass to 5. Players 5 and 1 go on offense, and play against 2, as shown in Figure 10.13c. Players 4 and 3 step out of the court.

Details to Teach and Underline

- Keep proper spacing between the two offensive players running in the two lanes outside the free-throw area.
- No fancy passes.
- Once he reaches the free-throw line extension, the ball handler must go straight to the basket, passing to his teammate only if the defender blocks the path to the basket.

214

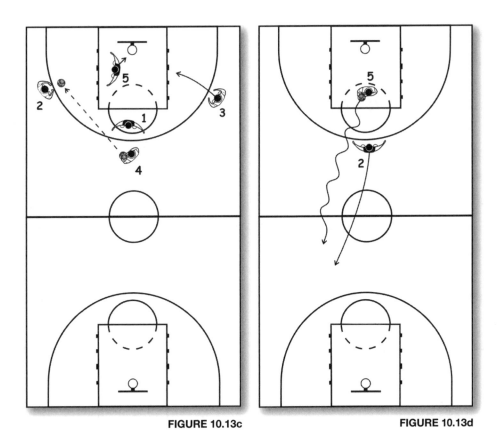

FIGURE 10.13c   FIGURE 10.13d

- Teach the defender to make defensive fakes to harass the offensive players as much as possible.
- All three players involved go for the rebound.

One-on-One: Let's assume that 2 has gone for the shot, either with a jump shot or a layup, so he becomes the defender, while 5 gets the ball and drives full court, while the passer, 1, steps out of the court.

Players 5 and 2 play one-on-one, as shown in Figure 10.13d. If the defender, 2, gets the ball, he attacks, driving to the opposing basket. The drill ends when one of the two players involved scores a basket. Then the other group steps in and starts the drill. Each group runs the drill for a certain number of times or for a given amount of time.

Details to Teach and Underline

- The offensive player must use the speed-dribble to drive to the opposing basket.

TWO–ON–ONE/FIVE–ON–FIVE DRILL

Aim

The aim of two–on–one/five–on–five drill is to practice all the possible fast-break situations, starting with the two-on-one, followed by the three-on-two, the four-on-three, the five-on-four, and, finally, the five-on-five. This is a very demanding drill that also helps the players get used to changing immediately from the offensive to the defensive, and vice versa.

Equipment

- 1 ball

Personnel

- The entire team

How to Run the Drill

The team is divided into two groups of five players each, one outside and along one baseline, and the other on the opposite baseline. The five players in each group are aligned with one player near the left corner, one near the left short corner, one under the basket, one near the right short corner, and one near right corner.

Two-on-One Fast Break: The player of one of the groups near the basket has the ball. The player in the middle of the line near the basket of the opposite group acts as a defender.

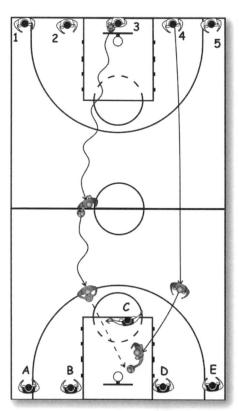

FIGURE 10.14a

As the coach shouts "Go," 3 and the player on his left, 4, sprint to the opposite basket, while C steps on the court and sets himself near the free-throw area in the middle of the court. Player 3 speed-dribbles on offense and plays two-on-one with 4, against C, as shown in Figure 10.14a.

Details to Teach and Underline

- Keep proper spacing between the two offensive players running in the two lanes outside the free-throw area.
- No fancy passes.
- Once he reaches the free-throw line extension, the ball handler must go straight to the basket, passing to his teammate only if the defender blocks the path to the basket.
- Teach the defender to make defensive fakes to harass the offensive players as much as possible.
- All three players go to the rebound.

Three-on-Two Fast Break: Once 3 and 4 have scored, or C gets the possession of the ball, B and D step on the court and play three-on-two against 3 and 4, who sprint to protect the opposite basket, as shown in Figure 10.14b.

Details to Teach and Underline

- Keep proper spacing between the three offensive players, wider than on the two-on-one.
- The two wings must go on the fast break, running in the lanes near the sidelines, with the ball handler in the middle lane

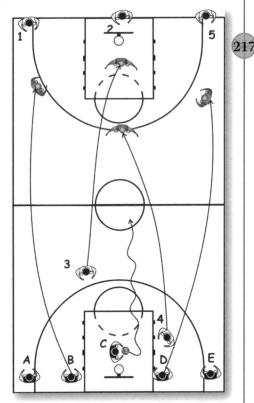

FIGURE 10.14b

217

of the court (or laterally, based on the type of fast break run in the game).

- No fancy passes.

- Once he reaches the three-point line, the ball handler must stop, keeping the dribble alive, and evaluate the best passing and shooting solution, while the two wings cut to the lane when they reach the free-throw line extension.

- Teach the defenders to make defensive fakes to harass the offensive players as much as possible.

- Two players go for the rebound and one is the safety.

Four-on-Three Fast break: Once B, C, or D have scored, or 3 or 4 get possession of the ball, 1 and 5 step on the court and play four-on-three with 3 and 4 against B, C, and D, who sprint to protect the opposite basket, as shown in Figure 10.14 c.

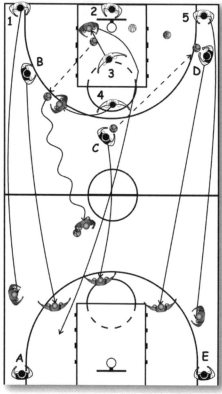

FIGURE 10.14c

Details to Teach and Underline

- Keep proper spacing between the four offensive players.

- The two wings must go on the fast break, running in the lanes near the sidelines, with the ball handler in the middle lane of the court (or laterally, based on the type of fast break run in the game), while the fourth player is the offensive trailer.

- No fancy passes.

- Once he is near the three-point line, the ball handler must stop, keeping the dribble alive, and evaluate the best passing and shooting solution.

- Teach the defenders to make defensive fakes to harass the offensive players as much as possible.

- Three players go for the rebound and one is the safety.

Five-on-Four Fast Break: Once 1, 3, 4, or 5 have scored, or B, C, or D get possession of the ball, A and E step on the court and play five-on-four with B, C, and D against 1, 3, 4, and 5, who sprint to protect the opposite basket, as shown in Figure 10.14d.

Details to Teach and Underline

- Keep proper spacing between the five offensive players.
- The two wings must go on the fast break, running in the lanes near the sidelines, and the ball handler is in the middle lane of the court (or laterally, based on the type

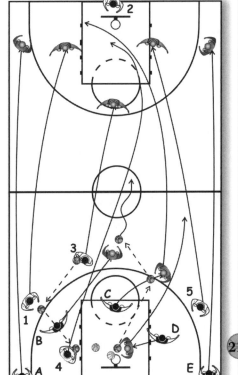

FIGURE 10.14d

of fast break run in the game), while the fourth and fifth players are the offensive trailers.

- No fancy passes.
- Once he is near the three-point line, the ball handler must stop, keeping the dribble alive, and evaluate the best passing and shooting solution.
- Teach the defenders to make defensive fakes to harass the offensive players as much as possible.
- Three players go for the rebound and two are the safeties, or in a different combination, based on the defensive transition philosophy of the team.

Five-on-Five Fast Break: Once A, B, C, D, or E have scored, or the defenders 1, 3, 4, or 5 get the possession of the ball, 2 steps on the court and plays five-on-five with 1, 3, 4, and 5 against A, B, C, D, and E, who sprint to protect the opposite basket, as shown in Figure 10.14e. Also in a situation with five offensive players against five defensive players, the offense must try to score before the defense is set. The drill is run for a certain number of times.

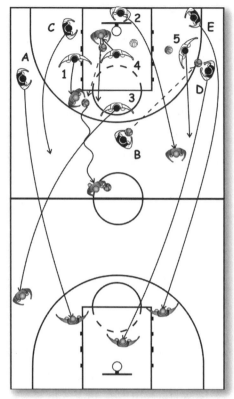

FIGURE 10.14e

Details to Teach and Underline

- Keep proper spacing between the five offensive players.
- The two wings must go on the fast break, running in the lanes near the sidelines, and the ball handler is in the middle lane of the court (or laterally, based on the type of fast break run in the game), while the fourth and fifth players are the offensive trailers.
- No fancy passes.
- Once he is near the three-point line, the ball handler must stop, keeping the dribble alive, and evaluate the best passing and shooting solution.
- Teach the defenders to make defensive fakes to harass the offensive players as much as possible.
- Three players go for the offensive rebound and two are the safeties, or in another combination, based on the defensive transition philosophy of the team.

11
Screen Drills

The screen, also called the "pick" or "drag», is the cornerstone of every offense. Screens can be on-ball (when set for the ball handler), or off-ball (when set for a teammate moving without the ball to get open for a pass). An offensive player who brings a screen must know how and at what angle to bring the screen. The screened player must be able to read the defense and react accordingly.

Working on screens requires attention to both timing and positioning for bringing the screen, using the screen, and reading what happens after the screen is made. A screen is not only a matter of size and speed, mixed with ball handling, but also involves many other details, from the options for the screened player or the options for the screener.

Teaching and practicing every type of screen used by your team and taking care of the details is of paramount importance to building an effective offense.

CONTINUOUS ON-BALL SCREEN DRILL

Aim

The aim of the continuous on-ball screen drill is to run two different types of screens, working on the side- and blind-screens. In this drill, the perimeter and inside players are mixed, so the inside players can practice on using and reading the screen, and the perimeter players get accustomed to bringing the screen.

Equipment

- 2 balls

Personnel

- The entire team
- A coach

How to Run the Drill

Divide the team into groups of three players, with one player on the left wing, one in the middle of the court with the ball, and one on the right. A coach is on the perimeter.

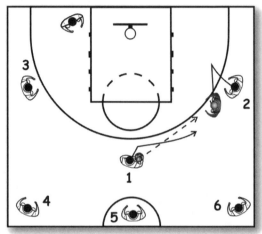

FIGURE 11.1a

Players 2 and 3 run and spot up at the wings, 3 on the left and 2 on the right. Player 1 passes the ball to 2, who has previously made a V cut before receiving the ball. After the pass, 1 fakes to go to the left, and then makes an on-ball side-screen to 2, as shown in Figure 11.1a.

Based on the coach's command, 2 will drive around the screen and go straight to the basket for a layup or a

FIGURE 11.1b

jump shot, or pass to 1, who has rolled to the basket, as shown in Figure 11.1b.

Player 1 can also flare away and receive the ball to shoot from outside, instead of rolling to the basket. Player 1 replaces 2 at the right wing spot.

Player 2 gets the rebound of his own shot, or the shot of 1. In the meantime, 3 has made a V cut, and 2 passes the ball to him, follows the pass and makes a blind screen for 3.

Based on the coach's command, 3 will drive to the basket for a layup or a jump shot, or pass to 2, who has rolled to the basket, as shown in Figure 11.1c.

Player 2 can also flare away and receive the ball to shoot from outside, instead of rolling to the basket. Player 2 replaces 3 at the left wing spot.

FIGURE 11.1c

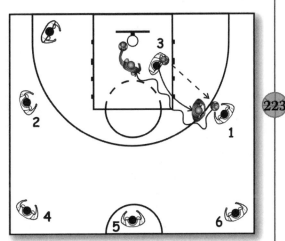

FIGURE 11.1d

Player 3 gets the rebound of his own shot, or the shot of 2. In the meantime, 1 has made a V cut, 3 passes the ball to him, follows the pass, and makes a blind-screen for 1.

Based on the coach's command, 1 will drive to the basket for a layup or a jump shot, or pass to 3, who has rolled to the basket, as shown in Figure 11.1d.

Player 3 can also flare away and receive the ball to shoot from outside, instead of rolling to the basket.

Player 1 gets the rebound of his own shot, or the shot of 3, and passes the ball to 2, who passes to 5, who runs a new session of the drill with 4 and 6.

This is the rotation: 2 goes to the end of 5's line, 1 to the end of 4's line, and 3 to the end of 6's line, as shown in Figure 11.1e. The drill is run for a certain number of repetitions per group or for a set amount of time.

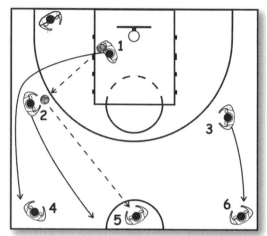

FIGURE 11.1e

Details to Teach and Underline

- *Screener:* Do not go straight to make the screen, but fake to go in the opposite direction, making a V cut.
- *Screened player:* Do not go straight to the screen, but set up the defender, making a couple of dribbles away from the screen.
- *Screener:* Screen perpendicular to the possible path of the defender, make a jump stop, and assume a wide stance.
- When driving to the basket, the ball handler must drive as close as possible to the screener's shoulder.
- Once the ball handler beats the defender, he must speed-dribble to finish to the basket.
- Players should drive with their heads up, in order to see the entire court, the screener, and their other teammates.

Variation

Add three defenders, who cover the offensive players initially at 50 percent, and then aggressively.

AWAY-FROM-THE-BALL SIDE-SCREEN-AND-ROLL SERIES DRILL

Aim

The aim of the away-from-the-ball side-screen-and-roll series drill is to create the proper flow of action between the screener and the screened player, and also to work on the roll and shooting of the screener after the screen.

Equipment

- 4 balls

Personnel

- The entire team

How to Run the Drill

The team is divided into four groups: one group with two balls is set in the left corner, one with two balls at the left-wing spot, one in the middle of the court, outside the three-point line, and one on the right-wing spot. A dummy defender is guarding the offensive player on the right wing spot.

Here are the different scoring options of the side screen-and-roll drill:

Screened player makes a jump shot at the free-throw-area/screener's roll to the basket: Player 1 fakes to go left, and then makes an away-from-the-ball side-screen on 2, who previously has set up the dummy defender, making a V cut. Player 2 cuts around the screen, runs at the left corner of the free-throw area, receives from 3, and makes a jump shot.

Right after the screen, 1 rolls to the basket, receives from 4, and shoots a layup or a power shot, as shown in Figure 11.2a. Players 1 and 2 get their own rebounds and go to the end of 4's and 3's

FIGURE 11.2a

lines, respectively, while 3 goes to the end of 1's line and 4 goes to the end of 2's line.

Screened player makes a jump shot out of the screen/screener's roll to the basket: Player 1 fakes to go left, and then makes an away-from-the-ball side-screen on 2, who previously has set up the dummy defender, making a V cut. Player 2 curls around the screen, receives the ball from 3 near the right corner of the free-throw line, and makes a jump shot.

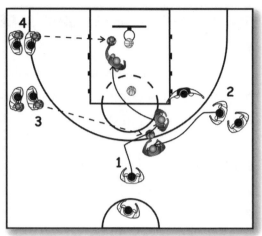

FIGURE 11.2b

226

Right after the screen, 1 rolls to the basket, receives from 4, and shoots a layup or a power shot, as shown in Figure 11.2b. Players 1 and 2 get their own rebounds and go to the end of the 4 and 3 groups, respectively, while 3 goes to the end of 1's line, and 4 to the end of 2's line.

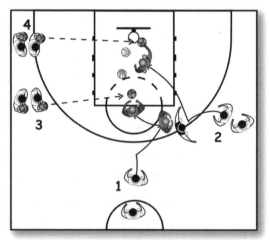

FIGURE 11.2c

Screened player's back-door cut/screener's roll and jump shot at the free-throw area: Player 1 fakes to go left, and then makes an away-from-the-ball side screen on 2, who previously has set up the dummy defender, making a V cut. Player 2 fakes to cut high and then makes a backdoor cut, receives from 4, and shoots a layup.

Right after the screen, 1 rolls to the free-throw area, receives from 3, and shoots a jump shot, as shown in Figure 11.2c. Players 1 and 2 get their own rebounds and go to the end of 3's and 4's lines, respectively, while 3 goes to the end of 1's line and 4 to the end of 2's line.

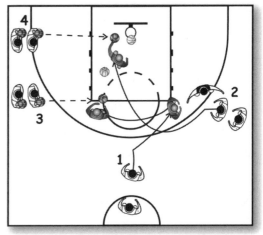

Screened player's curl around the screen—screener's roll and jump shot at free-throw area: Player 1 fakes to left, and then makes an away-from-the-ball side-screen on 2, who previously has set up the dummy defender, making a V cut. Player 2 curls around the screen, cuts in the lane, receives from 4, and shoots a layup.

FIGURE 11.2d

Right after the screen, 1 rolls to the free-throw area, receives from 3, and shoots a jump shot, as shown in Figure 11.2d. Players 1 and 2 get their own rebounds and go to the end of the 3's and of 4's lines, respectively, while 3 goes to the end of 1's line and 4 to the end of 2's line.

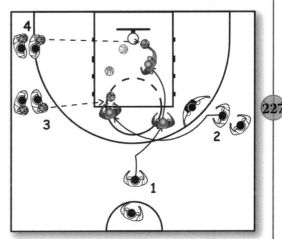

FIGURE 11.2e

Screen's fake of the screener and slip to the basket—jump shot of the screened player: Player 1 fakes to the left, and then goes toward 2 as if to make an away-from-the-ball side screen on 2, who previously has set up the dummy defender, making a V cut. But now, 1 slips to the basket, right before setting the screen, cuts in the lane, receives from 4, and shoots a layup.

Right after 1 has slipped and cut to the basket, 2 sprints to the free-throw area, receives from 3, and shoots a jump shot, as shown in Figure 11.2e. Players

227

1 and 2 get their own rebounds and go to the end of 4's and 3's lines, respectively, while 3 goes to the end of 1's line and 4 to the end of 2's line.

The drill is run until all the players have performed all the scoring options, both as a screener or as a screened player. The drill is also made on the right side.

Note: The drill can also be run with an away-from-the-ball high-screen-and-roll, with all the possibile scoring options, as shown in Figure 11.2f.

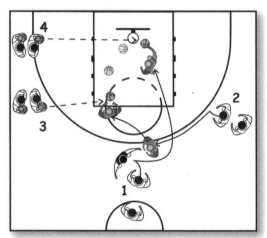

FIGURE 11.2f

Details to Teach and Underline

- *Screener:* Make a jump stop, assume a wide stance, and make the screen perpendicular to the possibile path of the defender.
- Screener and screened player: Change pace while rolling and cutting to the ball.
- *Screener:* Do not go straight to make the screen, but fake to go in the opposite direction making a V cut.
- *Screened player:* Do not go straight to the screen, but set up the defender, making a couple of dribbles away from the screen.
- *Screener:* Screen perpendicular to the possible path of the defender, make a jump stop, and assume a wide stance.
- *Screened player:* When driving to the basket, he must drive as close as possible to the screener's shoulder.
- *Screened player:* Once he beats the defender, he must speed-dribble to finish to the basket.
- *Screened player:* Drives with his head up, in order to see the entire court, the screener, and his three other teammates.

228

Variation

Another defender is added to the screener. The two defenders defend at 50 percent at the beginning, and then aggressively.

ON-BALL DOWN-SCREEN DRILL

Aim

The aim of the on-ball down-screen drill is for the screener and the screened player to practice the screen and shooting, at the same time.

Equipment

- 8 balls

Personnel

- The entire team
- Two coaches

How to Run the Drill

The team is divided into four groups, two on the left side of one half-court, and two on the left side of the the opposite half-court, while a coach is set at the wing position on each half-court with two balls.

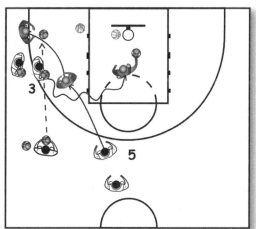

FIGURE 11.3a

Player 3's line, with two balls, is set in the corner, while player 5's line is set at about the three-point line. Player 3, starting with the ball at the triple-threat position, fakes to drive hard to the baseline, to set the defender, and then receives a down screen by 5, who has previously faked to go in the opposite direction.

Player 3 drives around the screen of 5 and finishes with a layup or a jump shot, as called by the coach, while 5 pops out to the corner, receives from the coach and shoots a jump shot, as shown in Figure 11.3a.

After the shot, 5 gets his own rebound, passes the ball to the coach and goes to the end of the line where he started the drill, while 3 gets his own rebound and goes to the end of the line where he started the drill. The drill is run for a certain number of repetitions or for a set amount of time, and is repeated on the right side of the court.

Details to Teach and Underline

- *Screener*: After the pass to the teammate to screen, take a couple of steps away from the ball, so you can then sprint to bring the screen, pop out, bend the knees, and show your hands as a target to the passer, indicating that you are ready to catch and shoot.
- *Screened player*: Set the defender with a couple of dribbles in the opposite direction, and then drive hard with a change of pace around the screen, shoulder to shoulder with the screener.

Here is a different action: 5 drives toward 3, makes a hand-off pass to 3, and screens him. Player 3 then drives around 5, finishing with a layup or a jump shot, as called by the coach, while 5 pops out in the corner, receives from the coach, and shoots a jump shot, as shown in Figure 11.3b.

After the shot, 5 gets his own rebound, passes the ball to the coach and goes to the end of the line where he started the drill, while 3 gets his own rebound and goes to the end of the line where he started the drill. The drill is run for a certain number of repetitions or for a set amount of time, and is repeated on the right side of the court.

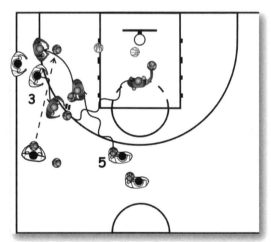

FIGURE 11.3b

Details to Teach and Underline

- *Screener:* Make the hand-off pass with two hands, protecting the ball with the body.
- *Screener*: Immediately after the hand-off pass and the screen, turn to the ball with knees bent, show your hands as a target to the passer, immediately ready to receive the ball from the coach, and catch and shoot.
- *Screened player:* Drive hard around the screen, shoulder to shoulder with the screener, with no more than two dribbles if shooting a layup.

Variation

Add two defenders on the screener and the screened player. They will first play defense at 50 percent, and then aggressively.

TWO-SHOT-AWAY-FROM-THE-BALL DOWN-SCREEN DRILL
Aim

The aim of the two-shot-away-from-the-ball down-screen drill is to practice the screen and the shooting at the same time of the screener and the screened player.

Equipment
- 5 balls

Personnel
- The entire team
- Two coaches

How to Run the Drill

The team is divided into four groups, one on the left wing with the balls, one in the middle of the court, one on the right wing, and one outside of the baseline. One coach is set on the perimeter, outside of the three-point line with a ball, and another with a ball is set opposite the right wing group.

Player 1 starts to dribble to the wing. At the same time, 2 makes a V cut and receives the ball from 1, while 3 cuts to the three-second lane and screens down on 4, who has previously set his dummy defender, X4, taking a couple of steps away from the ball.

Based on the head coach's command, "Curl," in this case, the defender will trail 4, so 4 curls around the 3's screen, cuts in the lane, receives from 2, and finishes with a layup.

Right after 4's curl, 3 pops out in the opposite direction of 4, receives from the coach on the right side of the court, and makes a jump shot, as shown in Figure 11.4a.

FIGURE 11.4a

The pattern of the drill is still the same, but this is another option for 4, based on the head coach's command. When the head coach shouts, "Flare," the defender, X4, goes over the screen, so 4 flares out, receives from 2, and makes a

FIGURE 11.4b

jump shot, while 3 rolls to the basket, receives from the coach on the left side, and finishes with a layup or a power shot, as shown in Figure 11.4b.

Players 4 and 3 grab their own rebounds and pass the balls from where they received the pass. Then, 4 goes to the end of 1's line, and 3 to the end of the baseline's line. Player X4 becomes the offensive player, and a player from the baseline line steps in and becomes the defender on X4. This is the rotation of the other players involved: 1 goes to the the end of 2's line, 2 to the end of 3's line. The drill is run until each player has done and has received a screen, or for a set amount of time. The drill is also repeated on the other side of the court.

Details to Teach and Underline

- Both offensive players must set up the screen, going in the opposite direction at the beginning where bringing and receiving the screen, and then changing pace and direction.
- When the screened player curls around the screener, he must curl shoulder to shoulder.
- Both players must always have the knees bent for all the actions in order to be ready to catch and shoot the ball immediately.
- On the flare, the screened player, in order to speed up his move and to give a signal of his intended move to the screener, will push himself off on the screener's back to help his movement in the new direction, and then jump away from the screener, always with knees bent.

233

Variation

Add a defender on the screener. The two defenders defend at 50 percent at the beginning, and then aggressively.

12
Rebounding

"*C*rash the boards!*"* How many coaches at the high school or pro level have used this rallying cry in their pep talks. Good offensive (and defensive) rebounding is essential to winning, because without it, the other team will have far too many chances to score, while your team will barely have any chance at all.

It is extremely important to teach and practice the rebound, and work, not only with the big men, but also with the perimeter players. Controlling the boards is often the difference between winning or losing a tight game, and rebounding drills will help your team be more dominant in the paint. Contrary to what most people think, rebounding is not about height or jumping ability: It has more to do with heart, determination, and aggressiveness. You can teach these skills by running rebounding drills at every practice.

The offensive rebound depends on a player's ability to sprint to the basket a split second after the shot is released, and above all, by the innate feeling to realize where the ball will fall after a shot.

The best example of a great rebounder is Dennis Rodman, the former NBA Detroit Pistons and Chicago Bulls forward. He is only 6' 7" and he was not an incredible jumper, but he was the best rebounder in the league for seven consecutive seasons, and he contributed to those teams winning five NBA titles.

Just as with any other fundamental, offensive rebounding must be practiced. The players must know how and when to move to get the offensive rebound, either when coming off the strong side or the help side of the court. They must work on anticipating the defenders' moves, before being blocked- (boxed) out, and master the different techniques of beating the block-out.

The following drills will help coaches achieve this target. Different from the other drills in this book, in almost all of these drills, defenders are added to get the offensive rebounders used to facing the block-out and teach them how to prevent the defenders from grabbing the rebound.

SIDE-TO-SIDE DRILL

Aim
The aim of the side-to-side drill is to work on rebounding while sprinting from one side of the three-second lane to the other, getting the rebound, and making the outlet pass.

Equipment
- 2 balls

Personnel
- The entire team

How to Run the Drill
The team is divided into four groups of players, two groups on each half-court. One group is behind the baseline and one group is at the wing spot. The players are paired with one player under the basket with the ball, and the other outside of the three-second lane.

Player 1, on the left side of the backboard, tosses the ball to the right side of the backboard, sprints to the other side, jumps as high as he can, grabs the rebound and makes an outlet pass to 2, who has previously made a V cut. Player 2 passes the ball back to 1, who tosses the ball to the left side of the backboard, while 2 sprints to the opposite side of the half-court. Players 1 and 2 repeat the same pattern, as shown in Figure 12.1.

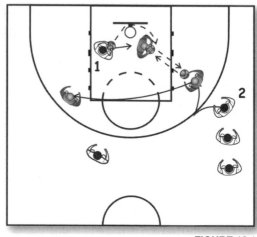

FIGURE 12.1

Player 1 repeats the same pattern for a certain number of repetitions or for a set amount of time. Then, 2 becomes the rebounder, 1 goes at the end of 2's line, and another player on 2's line becomes the receiver of the outlet pass.

Details to Teach and Underline

- Playing more aggressively on the rebound, as if in a game.
- When landing on the floor, the rebounder must protect the ball by holding it with one hand below and the other hand over top.
- Immediately turn the head toward the receiver, with the feet pointing toward him.
- Pass the ball to the receiver, who shows two hands as a target.
- While turning to receive the outlet pass, the receiver must have his back toward the baseline, not to the sideline, in order to see the entire court.
- The receiver must shout, "Ball" to the rebounder.

Variations

- Add a defender on the rebounder, who will first defend at 50 percent, and then aggressively.

- The player on the wing tosses the ball on the backboard, instead of the rebounder.

ROTATING SPOT DRILL

Aim

The aim of the rotating spot drill is to practice offensive rebounding while the defenders are moving in different spots.

Equipment

- 1 ball

Personnel

- The entire team
- A coach

How to Run the Drill

The team is divided into two groups of five offensive players with one ball, and five defenders, and a coach outside of the baseline. The offensive players are set outside and around the three-point line, and the defenders inside the three-point line.

Player 1 passes the ball to one of his teammates, to 3 in this case. As soon as the ball has been released from 1's hands, all the defenders rotate clockwise to the next spot, X1 to X3's spot, X3 to X5's spot, X5 to X4's spot, X4 to X2's, and X2 to X1's, and so on, while the offensive players keep their positions, as shown in Figure 12.2.

After a certain number of passes and rotations of the defenders, the coach

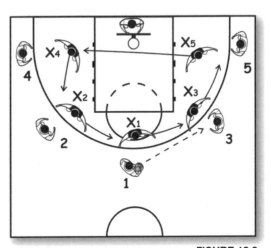

FIGURE 12.2

237

raises a hand, and the offensive player who has the ball shoots a jump shot. All the offensive players go to the rebound, while the defenders block-out. If the defense or the offense gets a rebound, they get 1 point. The first one who reaches 5 points wins, and the losers do sprints.

Details to Teach and Underline

- Don't go straight to the basket, but fake to go in one direction, and then move in the opposite direction.
- When faking, try to avoid physical contact with the defender, in order to beat him on a move.
- If blocked-out, use reverse, and "swim" with the arms, in order to go over the defender.
- Don't push the defender on his back, but use his back as a pivot, leaning on him with the shoulder, and then rotating.
- Try to anticipate where the ball will bounce off the rim or the backboard.
- Teach the players where the ball could drop, based on which spot of the court the shot is made and the height of the arc of the ball.

Variations

On every pass, the offensive players rotate with the defenders.

CALL-THE-SIDE DRILL
Aim

The aim of the call-the-side drill is to teach and work on the different techniques of how to go to the offensive rebound.

Personnel

- The entire team
- A coach

How to Run the Drill

The team is divided into two groups, lined and paired up, with one of the offensive and one of defensive players facing each other, and a coach behind the line of the defensive players. The two lines are four feet apart from each other.

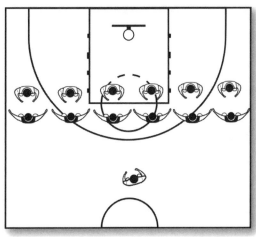

FIGURE 12.3

The coach raises his left or right hand, indicating which direction the offensive players should make the fake. They then go in the opposite direction, and, at the same time, he shouts either, "Reverse," or "Step over." The offensive players then must use one of the commands to go over the defenders to grab the imaginary offensive rebound, as shown in Figure 12.3. The defenders will block-out, at the beginning defending at 50 percent.

The drill ends after a certain number of repetitions or after a set amount of time. Then, the defenders become the offensive players, and vice versa.

Details to Teach and Underline

- Make the first, aggressive step in the direction called by the coach, with the knees bent.
- Don't push the defender away, but use his body as a pivot for the reverse, leaning on his back, in order to go over him.
- Keep arms high, to avoid being blocked by the defender, as well as to have a chance to "swim" over him.

Variations

The defenders block-out aggressively.

239

WAR-ON-THE BOARD DRILL

Aim

The aim of the war-on-the board drill is to practice offensive rebounding while moving around the lane, guarded by aggressive defenders.

Equipment

- 1 ball

Personnel

- The entire team

How to Run the Drill

Five offensive players, with one ball, are set around the lane, covered by five defenders. The offensive player with the ball passes it to one teammate, and then runs in the opposite direction of the pass and is replaced in the position he left.

FIGURE 12.4

After a minimum of three passes or more, the offensive player who receives the ball, shoots, and all ten players go to the rebound, as shown in Figure 12.4.

If the offensive players get the rebound, they try to score, and they get 1 point for the offensive rebound and another point if they score. If the defenders grab the rebound, they get 1 point. The first team that reaches 11 points wins, and the other team runs sprints.

Details to Teach and Underline

- Assume that every shot is missed, and move aggressively to get the rebound.
- Start to move as soon as the the ball is released from the hand of the teammate who has shot.
- Try to anticipate where the ball will bounce off the rim or the backboard.

240

- Teach the players where the ball could drop, based on which spot of the court the shot is made and the height of the arc of the ball.

Variations

The coach, set behind the baseline, raising one hand, will give the offensive players the signal to shoot.

IN-THE-WOOD DRILL

Aim

The aim in-the-wood drill is to practice going to the offensive rebound, while avoiding obstacles near and inside the three-second lane.

Equipment

- 2 balls
- 14 chairs

Personnel

- The entire team
- Two coaches

How to Run the Drill

The team is divided into two groups of five or more players, one group in each half-court set all around and outside of the three-point line, with a coach inside the three-point line holding a ball. Seven or more chairs are set randomly inside and around the three-point lane. Each player is numbered 1 to 5.

As the coach shoots the ball, he also calls one number, and the player with

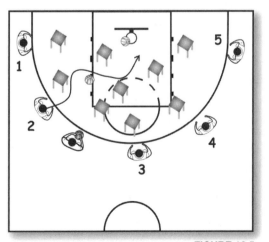

FIGURE 12.5

241

that number, 2 in this case, sprints to grab the rebound, running in between the chairs. He gets the ball, and passes it to the coach, who shoots again, and calls another number, as shown in Figure 12.5. The drill is run until all the players go to the rebound four times, or for a certain set time.

Details to Teach and Underline
- Watch the arc of the ball, but use peripheral vision to avoid the chairs.
- Go aggressively to the rebound as if in a game.

Variations
The players jog around the three-point line before sprinting to the rebound.

HALF-WHEEL DRILL
Aim
The aim of the half-wheel drill is to get the players used to going to the offensive rebound while moving, as the defenders block them out.

Equipment
- 2 balls

Personnel
- The entire team
- Two coaches

How to Run the Drill
The team is divided into two groups of six players each, one on each half-court. Each group is split with three defensive and three offensive players, and one ball. One pair of players is set in the middle of the half-court, and the other two in the left and right wing spots. A coach is in the corner.

Player 2 dribbles toward one of the wings, 1 in this case, and then he makes a hand-off pass to 1, who is going toward him. Then, the same hand-off pass is

made between 1 and 3. The three players continue to make a dribbling half-
wheel, always watching the coach, as
shown in Figure 12.6.

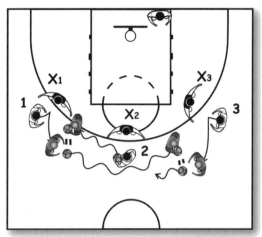

When the coach raises one hand,
the player with the ball shoots right
away, and all six players go to the rebound with the defenders, who block-
out the offensive players. If the defense
gets the rebound, they get 1 point, if
the offense gets the rebound and score,

FIGURE 12.6

they get 2 points. The group who reaches a certain score first wins, and the losers
run sprints.

Details to Teach and Underline

- This is a contest, but run under game conditions so the offensive and the players must not cheat, shooting "bricks" in order to run more quickly to the rebound, or blocking out, pushing and shoving.

Variations

At the coach's command, the player with the ball passes it to the coach, who
shoots, and then all six players go to the rebound.

ONE-ON-TWO DRILL

Aim

The aim of the one-on-two drill is to work under game conditions to get the offensive rebound and score.

Equipment

- 1 ball

243

Personnel

- The entire team
- A coach

How to Run the Drill

The team is divided into three groups of three players per group. One group is set in the middle of the half-court, one on the left- and one on the right-wing spots, while a coach with the ball is on the perimeter.

FIGURE 12.7

The coach shoots the ball, purposely misses the shot, and the first player of each group goes to the rebound. The player who grabs the rebound shoots, while the other two become the defenders and try to stop the offensive player from scoring without committing a foul, as shown in Figure 12.7

The three groups compete against each other, and the first group who scores three baskets wins. The losers must run sprints. If the defenders foul on the shooter, the shooter makes one free-throw, and, if he scores, he gets 1 point.

Details to Teach and Underline

- Once getting the rebound, don't bring the ball down, but jump back quickly with arms extended, and shoot immediately.
- If it is impossible to shoot immediately after the rebound, protect the ball with two hands on it and don't bring it below the chest.
- Keep a wide and strong stance to avoid being pushed away.

Variations

The coach passes the ball to one of the players, who shoots, and then he goes to the rebound with the other two players involved.

PASS-AND-SHOOT DRILL

Aim

The aim of the pass and shoot drill is to work on going to the offensive rebound from the strong- and weak-side of the court.

Equipment

- 2 balls

Personnel

- The entire team
- Two coaches

FIGURE 12.8

How to Run the Drill

The team is divided into groups of four players, and the drill is run on both half-courts. Two players from each group are the defenders and are set at the low-post positions, on the left and right side. Two offensive players are set outside of the three-second lane near the corners of the free-throw area, while a coach is under the basket with a ball.

The coach passes the ball to one of the offensive players, who shoots and purposely misses the basket. The two offensive players go to the rebound, and the two defenders block-out, as shown in Figure 12.8.

The action ends after a shot is made by the offensive players, or if the defenders grab the rebound. Then, the defenders become the offensive players, and the offensive players go to the end of the defenders' line, and two new defenders step in. The drill is run for a certain amount of made baskets or for a set amount of time.

Details to Teach and Underline

- Do not go straight to the basket, but fake to go in one direction and then move in the opposite direction.

- When faking, try to avoid physical contact with the defender, in order to beat him on a move.
- Keep the arms high to avoid being blocked by the defender, as well as having a chance to "swim" over him.
- If blocked-out, use reverse, and "swim" with the arms in order to go over the defender.
- Do not push the defender on his back, but instead use his back as a pivot, leaning on him with a shoulder, and then rotating.

Variations

The drill starts with the ball in the hands of one of the two offensive players, and they pass the ball to each other, while the defenders slide from the strong to the weak positions. When the coach raises one hand, the offensive player with the ball shoots, and the drill is run in the same way.

STRIP-THE-BALL DRILL

Aim

The aim of the strip-the-ball drill is to work on getting the offensive rebound and putting the ball back, while a defender tries to strip the ball away from the hands of the rebounder.

Equipment

- 2 balls

Personnel

- The entire team
- A coach

How to Run the Drill

The team is divided into groups of three players and the drill is run on both half-courts. One player with the ball, 1, is set near the free-throw area, one player, 2, is the rebounder and faces 1, while one defender, 3, is set under the basket.

Player 1 tosses the ball to the backboard, 2 turns and goes aggressively to grab the rebound, while 3 tries to strip the ball from the hands of 2, who must protect the ball and shoot right away, with a dunk or a power move, as shown in Figure 12.9.

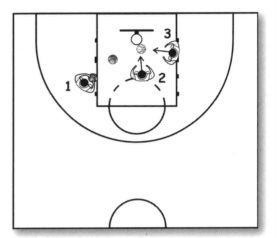

FIGURE 12.9

Details to Teach and Underline

- When landing on the floor, the rebounder must protect the ball by holding it with one hand below and the other hand over top.
- Once getting the rebound, don't bring the ball down, but jump back quickly with the arms extended, and shoot right away.
- If it is impossible to shoot immediately after the rebound, protect the ball the ball with two hands on it. Don't bring it below the chest and, when ready, make a power shot.

Variations

The defender plays an aggressive defense.

FOUR-ON-THREE DRILL

Aim

The aim of the four-on-three drill is to practice beating the defenders while they are blocking-out away from the ball, and grabbing the offensive rebound.

Equipment

- 2 balls

Personnel

- The entire team
- Two coaches

How to Run the Drill

The team is divided into two groups, one in each half-court. Each group is divided into four offensive players set around the perimeter, and three defenders set inside the three-second lane. A coach is outside of the court at the baseline under the basket, with one ball.

FIGURE 12.10

The coach passes the ball to one of the offensive players, to 1 in this case, who makes a jump shot, and stands there. Immediately, the three defenders sprint out of the lane and block-out the offensive players, who go to the offensive rebound, as shown in Figure 12.10.

If one of the offensive players grabs the rebound, he tries to score against the three defenders. If the offensive rebounder scores, the defense will play again against the same three players. However, if the defenders get the rebound, they go on offense, and vice versa. The drill is run until one of the two groups involved grab three rebounds, or after a set amount of time. If the players do not reach this goal, then another group of players steps in.

Details to Teach and Underline

- Don't go straight to the basket, but fake to go in one direction, and then move in the opposite direction.
- When faking, try to avoid physical contact with the defender in order to beat him on a move.

- If blocked-out, use reverse, and "swim" with the arms in order to go over the defender.
- Don't push the defender on his back, but instead use his back as a pivot, leaning on him with the shoulder, and then rotating.

Variations

Add another defender, set outside of the court near the baseline, who sprints to cover the shooter.

DOUBLE-DIGIT DRILL

Aim

The aim of the double-digit drill is to work on the reaction of the offensive players, who try to beat the defenders to the rebound.

Equipment

- 2 balls

Personnel

- The entire team
- Two coaches

How to Run the Drill

The team is divided into two groups, one in each half-court. Each group is divided into five offensive players, numbered from 1 to 5 and set around the perimeter, and two defenders set inside the three-second lane. A coach is on the perimeter, and a ball is set on the floor under the basket.

The coach calls a two-digit number,

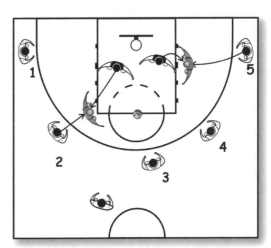

FIGURE 12.11

25, in this case. Players 2 and 5 sprint to the rim to grab the ball under the basket, while the two defenders block-out, as shown in Figure 12.11.

If the offensive players touch or grab the ball, they stay on offense, but, if the defenders block-out the offensive players for three seconds and stop them to get or touch the ball, they go on offense and vice versa.

Details to Teach and Underline

- Don't go straight to the basket, but instead fake to go in one direction, and then move in the opposite direction.
- When faking, try to avoid physical contact with the defender in order to beat him on a move.
- If blocked out, use reverse, and "swim" with the arms in order to go over the defender.
- Don't push the defender on his back, but use his back as a pivot, leaning on him with the shoulder and then rotating.

Variations

The coach with a ball calls the two-digit number and shoots.

TOUCH-THE-CHAIR DRILL

Aim

The aim of the touch-the-chair drill is to practice the rebound and outlet pass.

Equipment

- 2 balls
- 4 chairs

Personnel

- The entire team
- Two coaches

How to Run the Drill

The team is divided into two groups, one in each half-court. Each group is divided in pairs, one pair of players under the basket, and the other outside of the baseline. A coach is set in the lane, and two chairs are set outside the three-second lane on the left and right wing six feet away from the lane.

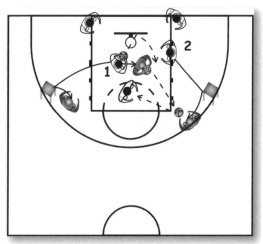

FIGURE 12.12

Player 1 tosses the ball to the backboard, while, at the same time, player 2 sprints to the chair on the right, touches it, and turns to the rebounder to receive the outlet pass from 1. Player 2 passes the ball to the coach, who tosses the ball to the backboard, while 2 sprints back to grab the rebound and makes an outlet pass to 1, who has sprinted to the chair, touched it, and has turned to the rebounder to receive the outlet pass from 2, as shown in Figure 12.12.

Each pair of players run the drill for a certain amount of time, and then another pair of players step on the court and run the drill.

Details to Teach and Underline

- Move aggressively to the rebound as if in a game.
- When landing on the floor, the rebounder must protect the ball by holding it with one hand below and the other hand over top.
- Immediately turn the head toward the receiver, with the feet pointing toward him.
- Pass the ball to the receiver, who holds up two hands as a target.
- While turning to receive the outlet pass, the receiver must have his back turned to the baseline, not to the sideline, in order to see the entire court.
- The receiver must shouts, "Ball" to the rebounder.

13

International Coaches' Top Drills

Until ten years ago, the United Stated totally dominated basketball, from the top to the youth international level competitions. Then the rest of the world started to close the gap. This was partially due to the fact that the U.S. coaches and players spent less time working on fundamentals and team play in favor of tactics and physical skills, such as jumping and speed.

In the rest of the world, accuracy in teaching the basics of the game, as well as practicing them, was and still is considered a priority. Now the tables have turned again in the United States, and foreign coaches are seen differently, and they are appreciated and studied.

In this last chapter of the book, we asked some international coaches to present their favorite offensive drills. Here are a few examples of how and why they work on a particular fundamental.

After reading this chapter, many of you will say, "I know this drill, and I adopted it a long time ago! What's new?" As we wrote at the beginning of this book, do not think these drills are magic tricks that will be able to change a normal player into a superstar. We think the message they, and we, would like to give is that simplicity is the keystone of a drill, and the repetitions and corrections are the real secrets. If the following coaches are so successful, aside from the fact that they had good players on their teams, it is because they worked hard at teaching and practicing the basics of the game, one of the secrets of a successful coach.

A final note: In this chapter you'll find the favorite drills of two Italian coaches. Please, do not think that, moved by patriotism, I included these two coaches, Ettore Messina and Sergio Scariolo, from my country. This was only dictated by the fact that these two coaches are now more "international," than others, have won competitions in every country in which they coached. In fact, some experts predict that one , or both of them, could be the first foreign coach in the NBA.

ETTORE MESSINA'S ONE-ON-ONE DRILL

Ettore Messina (Italy) is the head coach of the Spanish Club of Real Madrid. As a club coach, he won four Italian championships, three with Virtus Bologna and one with Benetton Treviso, and four Russian titles with CSKA Moscow. In the European competitions, he won four Euroleague titles, the top European championship for clubs– two with Virtus Bologna and two with CSKA Moscow, and one Saporta Cup with Virtus Bologna. As the coach of the Italian National Men's Team, he won a gold medal at the Mediterranean Games, and silver medals at both the European Championships and the Goodwill Games.

Aim

The aim of the one-on-one drill is to work in a game situation one-on-one and on the mental transition from offense to defense.

Equipment

- 1 ball

Personnel

- Six Players

How to Run the Drill

The team is divided into groups of five players each who work on the two half-courts. Each group is set in this way: two players, with a ball each, are in the middle of the court, one defender and one offensive player on the right-wing spot, in this case, and one player on the left-wing spot.

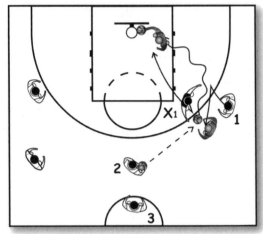

FIGURE 13.1a

The offensive player 1 makes a V cut, or another move to get open, and receives the ball from 2, while X1 plays an aggressive defense on 1. Player 1 attacks the basket and tries to beat X1, as shown in Figure 13.1a. Either on the made or missed shot, X1 grabs the ball and passes it to 3, the player in the

FIGURE 13.1b

middle of the court. Immediately after the shot, 1 runs to the opposite wing spot and plays defense on the offensive player on the left wing, as shown in Figure 13.1b. Player 3 passes the ball to the player on the left wing, who plays one-on-one with 1.

This is the rotation: the passer, 2, becomes the offensive player, the defensive player, X1, makes the pass to the line in the middle of the court and goes to the end of this line, and the offensive player, 1, becomes the defender on the opposite wing. The drill is run with the same pattern until all five players have played one-on-one, and ends after a certain number of one-on-ones of each player or after a set amount of time.

Details to Teach and Underline

- Be precise on every detail, both on offense and defense.
- Give the offensive player only few seconds to to get open.
- Make no more than a couple of dribbles to beat the defenders.

DIRK BAUERMANN'S SKIP-PASS AND PICK-AND-ROLL DRILL

Dirk Bauermann (Germany) has been the coach of the German Men's National Team since 2003. He won nine German men's championships, seven with Leverkusen and two with Bamberg, and also was the head coach in the Belgian top division with Ostende, and in the Greek top division with Patras. At the helm of the German National Team, he won the silver medal at the European Championship in 2005.

Aim

The aim of the skip-pass and pick-and-roll drill is to teach the fundamentals of the pick-and-roll and all its different offensive options.

Equipment

- 1 ball per player

Personnel

- The entire team
- A coach

How to Run the Drill

The team is divided into two lines of inside and perimeter players, both on the same side of the court. The inside players, each with a ball, are lined up at the low-post spot, and the perimeter players, each with the ball, at the wing spot. A coach is set on the opposite wing spot, on the right, in this case.

The first player on the inside players' line, 4, makes a skip-pass to the coach and runs to make a pick for the perimeter player, 2, who dribbles around the pick. Right after the pick, the inside player rolls to the basket, receives a bounce-pass from the perimeter player, and shoots. After the pass to the inside player, the perimeter

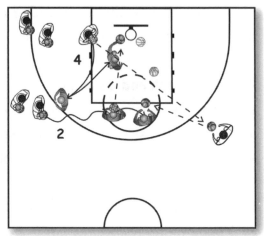

FIGURE 13.2

player goes toward the coach, receives the ball, and shoots a jump shot, as shown in Figure 13.2.

After four minutes or after a certain number of made shots, the perimeter player makes a jump shot coming off the pick, while the inside player, who has rolled to the basket, receives the ball from the coach and shoots under the basket.

Details to Teach and Underline
- Teach the inside players to roll properly to the basket.
- The perimeter player must dribble over the pick, brushing his shoulder with the shoulder of the picker.
- The bounce-pass must be hard, so the perimeter player can easily catch the ball.

Variation
The two offensive players run different shooting options, such as popping-out, slipping the pick, and so on.

SARUNAS MARCIULIONIS'S THREE-LINE SHOOTING DRILL

Sarunas Marciulionis (Lithuania) was one of the first foreign players to play in the NBA. In 1992, after a good career with Golden State, Seattle, Sacramento, and Denver, as well as with the Russian National Team, he established the Marciulionis Basketball School, in Vilnius, Lithuania, where young players could work to improve their basketball skills. Many top Lithuanian players have come out of this institute to play in different foreign championships.

Aim

The aim of the three-line shooting drill is to improve shooting under defensive pressure and in a contest.

Equipment

- 3 balls

Personnel

- Nine players

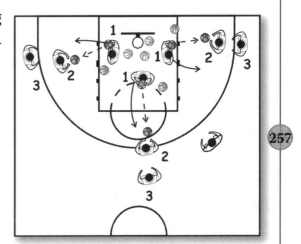

FIGURE 13.3a

How to Run the Drill

The players are divided into three squads of three players, one set in the middle of the court, one in the left corner, and one in the right. Each squad has a ball.

The drill starts with players 1 of each squad under the basket, each with a ball. Player 1 passes the ball to his teammate, 2, follows the pass, and harasses the shooter, as shown in Figure 13.3a. The shooter, 2, goes to the

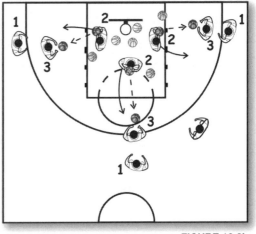

FIGURE 13.3b

rebound and passes to player 3 on his line and runs to harass him while he is shooting. Then player 1 of each squad goes to the end of the line, as shown in Figure 13.3b.

Each player calls out the number of his made shots. Each squad competes against the other two, and each player competes against the other two teammates on the same squad. The drill ends after a certain number of made shots or a set amount of time.

Details to Teach and Underline

- Be ready to shoot immediately after receiving the ball, with knees bent, the feet pointed to the basket, and the hands at chin level.
- When shooting, keep the elbow aligned with the shoulder and follow through with the shot.

258 ### Variation

The players make one or two dribbles or take a step-back before shooting.

SERGIO SCARIOLO'S "DOUBLE"-SHOT HIGH PICK-AND-ROLL DRILL

Sergio Scariolo (Italy) is the head coach of the Spanish Men's National Team and of the Russian Club Team, Khimki Moscow. He won an Italian top league title with Pesaro and two Spanish top league titles, one with Real Madrid and one with Malaga. With the Italian Armed Force National Team, he won the World Armed Forces Championship.

Aim

The aim of the "double"-shot high pick-and-roll drill is to practice an offensive play that we use a lot during the course of the game, working on the picker and picked player's shots.

Equipment

- 1 ball for each perimeter player
- 1 ball for the coach

Personnel

- The entire team
- A coach

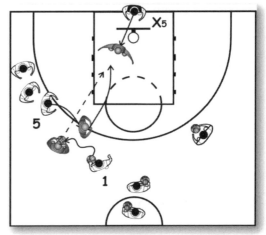

FIGURE 13.4a

How to Run the Drill

The players are divided into two groups, one group of perimeter players, each with a ball in the middle of the court, and one of inside players under the basket. A coach with a ball is set at the free-throw line extension.

The drill starts with an inside player, 5, outside of the three-point line, who picks-and-rolls for player 1. Right after the pick, another one on the inside player line, X5, steps into the court and sets himself near the basket, acting as a defender against 5, who has rolled to the basket and received the pass. Player

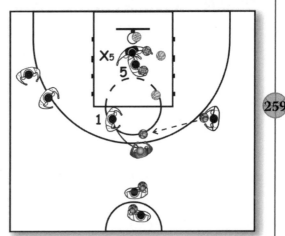

259

FIGURE 13.4b

5 goes to the basket with a power move, as shown in Figure 13.4a. Right after the pass to 5, 1 runs to the middle of the court to receive the ball from the coach and shoot a three-pointer, as shown in Figure 13.4b.

This is the rotation: X5, the defender on 5, gets the rebound, passes the ball to the coach, and runs outside of the three-point line, in order to play a pick-and-roll with the next player in the group in the middle of the court, and 1 gets his own rebound, and goes to the end of his line.

Details to Teach and Underline

- Make a couple of dribbles to set up the pick.
- Teach the picker to assume a wide stance and roll, pivoting in the proper way.
- While turning around the pick, the ball handler must brush the shoulder of the picker.

Variation

We work on the same drill, but now as a pick-and-pop option.

DUSAN IVKOVIC'S FOUR-ON-FOUR "SHELL" DRILL

Dusan Ivkovic (Serbia) is the head coach of the Serbian Men's National Team. At the top level club, he won a Yugoslavian title with Partizan Belgrade, two Greek titles, one with Paok Athens and one with Olympiacos Athens, and three Russian titles with CSKA Moscow. At the European club competitions, he won a Euroleague with Olympiacos, a Saporta Cup with AEK Athens, a Korac Cup with Partizan Belgrade, and an ULEB Cup with Dynamo Moscow. At the helm of the Yugoslavian Men's National Team, he won a gold at the FIBA World Championship and three gold medals and one silver medal at the FIBA EuroBasket Championships.

Aim

The aim of the four-on-four "shell" drill is to work on spacing and on finding the best offensive solutions after a dribble penetration and a pass to the low post.

Equipment

- 1 ball

Personnel

- Eight players

How to Run the Drill

Four players are on offense, two on the left- and right-wing spots, and two on the left and right corners, and four defenders are matched up with the four offensive players.

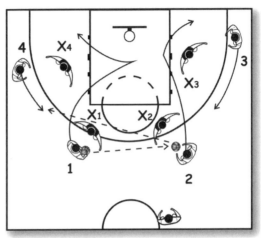

FIGURE 13.5a

One of the offensive players, 1, has a ball and starts to pass to one of his teammate, 2, in this case. Then, 2 passes to another teammate, 4, in this case, as shown in Figure 13.5a.

After a certain number of passes, minimum three or at the coach's command, the player with the ball, 3, in this case, penetrates in the lane from the wing position.

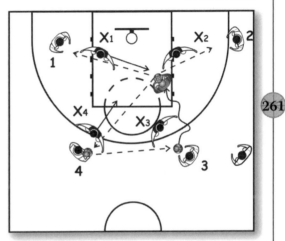

FIGURE 13.5b

Based on the reaction of the defender, X1, on the help side, the ball handler, 3, will decide which is the best offensive solution: to pass to 1, to 2, or to 4, as shown in Figure 13.5b.

Now the offensive players pass the ball and screen each other. Player 5, in this case, passes the ball to 4 and screens for 3, then player 4 passes to 3 and screens for 2, as shown in Figure 13.5c.

At some point, after a certain numbers of screens or at the coach's command, the ball is passed from the wing, 3, in this case, to the low-post, 5, who penetrates. He can penetrate along the baseline or in the middle of the three-second lane, and he will decide the best solution, based on the reaction of the defenders. If he

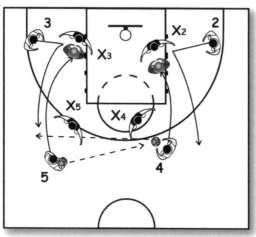

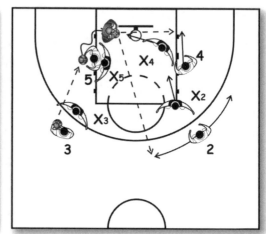

FIGURE 13.5c

FIGURE 13.5d

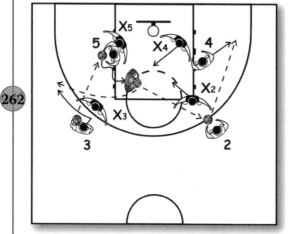

FIGURE 13.5e

penetrates on the baseline, he can pass to 4 or 2, who has spotted up, as shown in Figure 13.5d. If he penetrates in the middle of the lane, he can pass to 2 and 2 to 4, or also to 3, if X3 jams the lane, as in Figure 13.5e.

JOSÉ VICENTE "PEPU" HERNANDEZ'S OUTLET PASS WAVE DRILL

After eleven seasons as head coach with Estudiantes Madrid, one of the best Spanish league clubs, José Vicente "Pepu" Hernandez (Spain), guided the Spanish Men's National Team to a gold medal at the FIBA World Championships in 2006, and to a silver medal at the FIBA EuroBasket in 2007.

Aim

The aim of the outlet pass wave drill is to practice the outlet pass to start the fast break, as well as to improve conditioning,

Equipment

- 1 ball

Personnel

- Twelve players

How to Run the Drill

The team is divided into three groups of four players. Two players, each with a ball, are set in the middle of the court, and two players are near the three-second lane—one on the left side and the other on the right.

Player 1 passes the ball to 3, who has popped out of the three-point line, then cuts in the lane, and receives the ball back from 3, as shown in Figure 13.6a.

Player 1 tosses the ball to the backboard, grabs the rebound, and passes again to 3, who has run to the corner. Then 1 sets himself near the lane. At the same time, 2, the second player in the middle of the court, goes to right-wing spot, receives from 3, and passes the ball to 4, who popped out to the three-point line. After the pass to 4, 2 goes high to the wing spot, as shown in Figure 13.6b.

After the pass to 4, 2 cuts in the lane, receives the ball from 4, tosses it on the backboard, grabs the rebound, and passes again to 4, who has run to the corner. Then 2 sets himself near the lane, as shown in Figure 13.6c. The

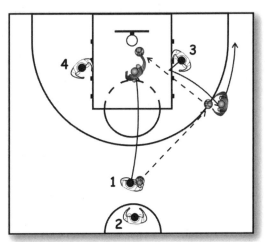

FIGURE 13.6a

drill continues in the same way, and is run for 20 to 40 seconds, because it requires high intensity. Then, another four players step in.

Details to Teach and Underline

- Execute all the passes, cuts, and rebounds with extreme accuracy.
- Request perfect coordination from all the players.
- The receiver must always show his hand as a target for the passer. Cut to the spot to receive the ball at the proper time, not too early or too late.
- Pass very quickly after grabbing the rebound.

Variation

At a certain point at the coach's command, the four players run the fast break and score on the opposite basket.

FIGURE 13.6b

FIGURE 13.6c

ACKNOWLEDGMENTS

I love basketball!

After forty years of basketball played (at a very low level in my home town of Cremona, Italy); coaching at the youth and Division II level, after having organized and attended many basketball camps and clinics all over the world, after having written four technical books on basketball published in the United States and Italy, and after having watched a few thousand games, in person and on television, I still find basketball to be fascinating.

Basketball is a mix of power, finesse, intelligence, team play, quickness, and many other aspects that I find in no other team sport. The perfectly executed fundamentals, the different offenses and defenses, the exciting fast breaks, the thundering dunks and blocked shots, the deft assists, and the final shot that beats the buzzer have all been a big part of my life.

When people ask me what I do for a living, I tell them that I was lucky to have fallen in love many years ago with this wonderful game—and then basketball gave me a profession. I started out years ago and continue today as a journalist covering basketball around the world. Later, I began working in sports marketing, helping to organize basketball tournaments, camps, and clinics.

This book would not have been possible without the experience and assistance of many people, but if I were to name them all I would fill more pages than I have been allotted.

I especially want to thank two basketball experts who are no longer with us. Chuck Daly, the legendary NBA and Dream Team coach, first introduced me to the college game many years ago, and then brought me into the inner sanctum when he became an NBA head coach. Claudio Papini was another mentor, a fantastic teacher of fundamentals, and had he ever coached at the high school level in the United States he would have been one of the very best.

Many thanks to former college and NBA standout coaches, including Lou Carnesecca, Bob Zuffelato, Dean Smith, Mike Fratello, Jack Ramsay, and Hubie Brown, an unbelievable teacher of basketball fundamentals.

When it comes to active coaches, there are many who gave advice and their favorite drills. I acknowledge with deep gratitude the "wizards-of-the-chairs drills," Kevin Sutton, head coach of Montverde Academy, and assistant coach of the U.S. Under 16 Men's National Team, and Kevin Eastman, assistant coach of the Boston Celtics and a great proponent of fundamentals. Thanks also to Raphael Chillious, assistant coach of Washington University, Ganon Baker, an unbelievable demonstrator of fundamentals, and Steve Smith of Oak Hill Academy, one of the best high school coaches in the United States. Going international, I want to thank Ettore Messina, Sergio Scariolo, and Carlo Recalcati, all great Italian coaches; Moncho Monsalve from Spain, as well as all the other international (and American) coaches I had the privilege to talk to and watch as they ran their practice sessions over the years. They have inspired and instructed me, and I will never forget that.

A special thanks Ron Martirano of McGraw-Hill, who trusted and supported me throughout this project; to Lisa Cavallini, the creative art director of this book, who has worked with me for a decade at *Giganti del Basket*, the Italian technical basketball magazine, and *FIBA Assist*, the official technical magazine of the International Basketball Federation; Raffaele Imbrogno, the "king of basketball diagrams;" and Gastone Marchesi and Filippo Arduino, who also greatly helped me with this project.

I give a special thanks to the sport of basketball, which has provided so much fun, excitement, and a way of life. But most of all, I owe a million thanks to my precious "point guard," Ornella, who is my second, sorry, my first true love.

ABOUT THE AUTHOR

Giorgio Gandolfi is the editor-in-chief of *FIBA Assist*, the technical magazine of FIBA, the International Basketball Federation, and of *Giganti del Basket*, the Italian basketball magazine for coaches. He has been a member of the Italian Basketball Coaches Association since 1974 and he was an European consultant for the National Basketball Coaches Association.

He coached at the youth level and was assistant coach at Division II and III. He ran the first ever NBA camp in Europe, and also organizes camps and clinics in Italy. While working on promotion and events with Converse Europe, he organized camps and clinics all over the Europe, in China and Argentina.

He is the author of three technical basketball books in the US: *NBA Coaches Handbook* and *NBA Coaches Playbook*, both with the NBA Coaches Association, and Hoops–*The Official National Players Association Guide for Playing Basketball*, with the NBA Players Association. He also published four books on basketball in Italy.

Photo by Ricciardo Cecchi

266